In October last year I approached the governmental agency that provides drug counselling because my 32 year old daughter had become addicted to methamphetamine. I had seen her through the teenage years, her early twenties, the danger years. At 30 she slipped into meth use and very quickly developed habitual use costing thousands a week. I watched as her body became skeletal, as her limbs twisted, her face become hard like stone and her mind became tortured only thinking how she could get more. Her normally good judgement, nice demeanour and caring way was replaced with desperate, bizarre and often violent fragmented actions and thoughts. The night before Christmas, she stole the safe from my office and fled.

I went to get help and was told there was nothing they could do. Their advice was that I got rid of her from my business and my life. For my information there were businesses going down every day because of key people using methamphetamine. They could help me and put me in touch with a group of family members of drug users, that they could only help my daughter when she was ready.

I did attend a group and they did give me strategies to function with some reason again. The strong message they gave was to let go of her and keep myself and business safe. They didn't seem to know much about meth use or what the likelihood of a recovery would be and thought that if she could stop using she may be able to live a semi- normal life again but she wouldn't be the same as she was.

I'm now delighted to tell you I have my clear thinking caring daughter BACK. Complete with ethics and morals.

In January this year I was introduced to Christina Stroud as someone that could help my daughter, they met, she intervened, she cared, she didn't agree with waiting until my daughter was ready. Using her system, Christina was determined my daughter would recover completely. She could tell me at all times what stage she was at and what stage she would be at next and was right every time. There was no force, no rehab centre, just smart strategies and clever techniques that made it look simple.

Family and friends don't want or need to be told to let go, that these meth users are untouchables, 21st century lepers. As parents and family of course we feel responsible and so we should - they are loved members of our families. Methamphetamine has left them mentally and physically impaired so they require intervention and assistance, the same way someone with two broken legs can't walk to the hospital or someone with dementia needs someone to make decisions for them.

My daughter now admits she never wanted to give up but from the first day she met Christina using meth was never the same and it was easy for her to let it go. She didn't feel sick or have to sleep for days when she stopped. She says it was EASY. Please read this book and find solutions, stop your pain and feel comforted knowing that you now have a pretty good chance of success in getting back your loved one.

Mother of 33 year old female

Some 12 months ago I had the privilege of meeting Christina Stroud, through an introduction by a mutual friend and one who also shared a similar journey to myself in the heart-wrenching discovery that beloved family member was addicted to the drug methamphetamine.

Christina's energy and passion for her chosen profession, her wisdom and knowledge of the behaviour and mind of the meth addict has impressed us and been a source of great encouragement in our understanding the effect this addiction is having on our family - knowing now that a path for recovery and eventual freedom from meth is viable - our grandson is recovering well.

Grandmother of 18 year old

Christina's system as described in the book takes a proactive, effective and holistic stance. There is no reason to feel powerless, either as a user or family of one because it is fixable if you use the strategies offered. I know because we had a family member who needed help. It worked for us- it saved his life.

Parents of a 35 year old male

When our son left his wife and three children out of the blue we were shocked and then we discovered why- he had started using methamphetamine four years previously. He was erratic, aggressive and was at the point of no longer being able to function before we found out. Most concerning was the fact he didn't seem to care. The wisdom contained in this book helped us as an extended family cope with the pain and helplessness we felt. It provided us the words to say and the actions to take to help our beloved father, husband and son come back to us, and he did.

Family of 43 year old male

Thank you for letting me preview this wonderful book- I am a health professional and quite frankly had started to believe there was no hope- and this was an epidemic that was uncontrollable and unstoppable. Knowledge is King!!! We can do something.

Community worker

I loved this book. I believe I can use it with my not clients who use methamphetamine but those who abuse alcohol. It was simple, intelligent and very kind. It provided all the information, tools, and exercises that are normally never revealed – I think this book will change the way we see recovery from drug use. As a drug counsellor I feel a great big boost of energy and a revival of my spirit.

Drug Counsellor for 17 years

We have an epidemic. As a father of teenagers I am afraid for them and their friends. Now I have plenty of stories that will serve as a graphic lesson as to why they need leave this drug alone.

Dad of four

In Hawaii, meth use is being called the biggest social catastrophe ever known. I have lost friends who should have known better- this ugly drug has left them in jail and with convictions, broken relationships and like myself wounded friends and family. If I can help just one after reading this book I'll give it my best. This is a drug like no other , we must all help.

Friend

You Are More Than This Will Ever Be

methamphetamine: the dirty drug

CHRISTINA STROUD

New York

Zealand Drug Detection Agency for their support. Thank you Jas, for the rest and recreation I enjoyed in New York before I took this challenge on.

Whenever I mentioned I was writing this book about methamphetamine, I was astonished by the response—everybody knows somebody who is trapped in its use. I know this will help. I have had resounding success, and without any doubt my clients have all agreed: they were in trouble and didn't know where to turn, and now they have their lives back.

I want to acknowledge everyone reading this book; thank you for doing me the honor.

DEDICATION

I want this book to offer condolence and speak hope to mothers and daughters, to tell the truth to fathers and sons, to support broken-hearted lovers who have become victims, to stop the hurt to children, and to hug those shaking in anger, fear, and pain in their first faltering steps toward a better life for themselves.

My heart is full.

Contents

methamphetamine: not now, not ever.

You Are More Than This Will Ever Be

You Are More Than This Will Ever Be will alarm, inspire and motivate you. It is written as a self-help book for anyone who is using methamphetamine and needs help to stop. Using the system, *you will coach yourself out of using the drug* and into a life of freedom. If you have attempted to stop your methamphetamine use before and it didn't work, that is simply because you didn't have the strategy and the steps- Now you do.

The tools in *You Are More Than This Will Ever Be* are also a guide for families and friends of methamphetamine users who decide to help and need to know how. The first part of the book Section 1 is made up of case studies and stories from my experience in working with users. While names have been changed I chose a wide scope of clients so to capture the diversity of the situations and wide ranging backgrounds of the people who use this drug.

Section 2 gives you a complete tool kit, to coach yourself or others through to freedom from methamphetamine use. Section 3 is an explicit and thorough guide for you as a coach working with a client. It has explanations about how and why the specific strategies work. *There are things to say and the reasons for saying them to help the person using find a reason not to.*

This book addresses the pain of becoming a victim to a loved ones use. I hope it will provide solace and reason to something that doesn't make any sense. *You Are More Than This Will Ever Be* offers an you a clearer understanding of the situation as it is, and an increasing confidence in the fact *it does have not have to stay that way.*

It can be used to gain information and awareness about the problem that the supply and demand of methamphetamine causes. You may be a health care professional, teacher, therapist or social worker and want some specific structure to working with users. You are welcome to use my system, please provide any feedback that you have in the way of success stories.

You Are More Than This Will Ever Be is guaranteed to challenge traditional thinking. It is a vital resource for those concerned that their children will be tempted with the decision as they get older- and because the use of methamphetamine on a global scale has escalated, that is virtually inevitable.

I am training coaches now to work this with system; you will find more information at www.hopeofanation.net. I will welcome your inquiry.

INTRODUCTION

Somewhere beyond right doing and wrong doing,
there is a field; I'll meet you there.

—RUMI

Gaining experience with methamphetamine users was unintentional, but what I do has worked with many users, as you will see in the stories I describe. I hope I can offer the same strategies through *You Are More Than This Will Ever Be.* I did not originally have any interest in working with methamphetamine users. To my practical, simple mind, drugs are bad and they will end up abusing you and ruining your life, so I don't touch them.

This book is a guide for a user who wants to stop, and it provides information and education for those who want to know more or fear they know somebody who needs help. *You Are More Than This Will Ever Be* is for anybody who is socially aware and wants some hope. This book is based on case studies of users I have worked with, of which I have had many, so I used a sprinkling of stories—I hope I captured enough for most people to relate to.

Methamphetamine has had a different effect compared to most drugs; hence its reputation as "the lying lady." She promised you so much and will deliver you so little, but you keep going back for more.

The use of methamphetamine is destroying lives like no other drug before—sure, there has always been drug use, but nothing as insidious as this drug. Methamphetamine steals more than it will ever offer. Once you start using, *if you are without the will and strategy to stop,* the nature of the drug will get you right back again: it destroys your brain; makes you aggressive and violent, alternatively depressed and hopeless; and leaves your judgment impaired. Using drugs limits your freedom—*methamphetamine will steal your soul.*

While this book is focused on my work with recovery from methamphetamine, of course it is transferable knowledge and can be used to address any other drug or alcohol or undesirable behavior that is causing you grief.

Methamphetamine has become the scourge that it is because people who use it start making it to keep their own supply up. It is easily accessible, is relatively cheap, and attracts people from all walks of life, status, and race because most insidiously it promises a shortcut to success.

When people use methamphetamine, they believe they are inspired, charismatic, and unstoppable and can move mountains. The truth is there is no shortcut, but those things are a right and available to every one of us—you can have the things you seek, but you have to do the work.

My reasons for this work started as a consequence of my business, and my motivation is inspired by a personal one: I had a friend who took his life after being arrested for possessing methamphetamine. The humiliation he faced, the loss of his job, and the scandal for his family proved insurmountable to him. He had always smoked dope, but as the trend developed he started using methamphetamine (I will refer to methamphetamine as "meth" also). As he suffered and more of the effects of his drug use took their toll—he was drinking heavily as well—he became increasingly isolated and depressed.

He was a sensitive soul. He would binge on methamphetamine. His mind would race, and he would enjoy the increased drive and feelings of invincibility—until it was over, and then he would seek solace in the opiate, calming effects of marijuana. This must have worked at first, but soon this emotional chaos led him to the only answer to his life he had left. The more he needed help, the better he became at avoiding it: after he was arrested and charged, and while waiting for his court appearance, he hung himself, and a community, which he will never know cared the way it did, grieved for him.

I spent an unreasonable time feeling guilty about his suicide. I had noticed how miserable and alone he was. I suspected things weren't going well for him and kept meaning to speak to him. I wasn't astute enough to recognize the signs without doubt, and he would have lied at first anyway. The highly illicit nature of the drug, his professional standing, and the consequences of using methamphetamine meant I felt it a forbidden subject and difficult to ask him about after all, I couldn't know for certain. That meant he couldn't ask. He was in too deep to help himself, to ask for the help he needed, and he chose the harshest penalty. I know I could have helped. *By asking him what was wrong, anyone could have helped.*

His tragic death served as a lesson to many; the pain of his death was felt deeply by many. If only he had known. As I write this, I still cry at the waste of his life. Thank you, my friend, for helping me care enough, this was a promise I made to you, to work to stop the supply and demand of this filthy drug. I hope this book does that and inspires you, the reader to join our global campaign. Please go to www.hopepfanation.net for more information as to what else you can do to be involved with stopping the kind of pain that was felt by my friend,his family and community.

My business is in success and high performance. I started a coaching company fifteen years ago. I developed the tools I teach. They are all based on scientific theory and psychological concepts I learned studying and applying psychology.

What I haven't mentioned is how I was a victim to a married couple who were both using methamphetamine at the time, pulling off scams for money, the people they enlisted, some of them unknowingly, and the system that supported them.

They introduced themselves into my business when I had just begun this work, which probably left me a little vulnerable. It's pretty obvious in hindsight, and I would like to say I learned a valuable lesson, but I just feel ripped off and don't believe justice has been done. The extent of their planning was incredible, with me completely unaware. The justice system hasn't yet caught up to the impact this drug makes, to the extent users will go to get the money they want. But I'm leaving that story for my next book, *My Spirit Song*, which is about eight life lessons.

When the heart weeps for what it loses,
the Spirit sings for what it finds.
—SUFI

Introduction

Over the years I have trained hundreds of coaches and clients from all walks of life and enjoyed the privilege of getting to know in-depth how people think, what motivates them, what stifles them, and what it is that sabotages our success. Without exception every living person is challenged in life—some more than others. Everyone has expectations; some are more rewarding than others. All of us have suffered defeat, uncertainty, pain, and loss along with accomplishment, success, and happiness.

I started seeing more and more corporate clients and business owners whose lives and businesses were not working. Often they had been sent to me because others knew something was wrong; among typical effects were poor results due to increasingly erratic behavior and poor decisions, displays of temper, and agitation toward others. Their performance was being affected, they soon revealed they were using methamphetamine, and as a consequence we tackled their drug-use behavior. Very quickly they put their lives back on track—without criminalization and never without consequence, but with the least possible damage.

Methamphetamine is like no other drug in what it will do to the way you think and to the things you will do once it has you in its grip.

The sooner you stop using methamphetamine, the sooner your life will be meaningful again. Are you guaranteed a life without further pain? Not likely, but with what you know now you can help others avoid the trap you fell into yourself, because living as a drug user is a poor second to living without the curse of the abuse that drugs create.

This book will give you a way to stop using, as well as strategies for coping when things get difficult (because there will be times that are difficult) – and the drug has played a part in how you dealt with things in the past- however, this can be a simple process too- it's up to you.

My client list grew, and with people who had tried already to give up, been through rehab (sometimes more than once), and so far had not managed to break the chains that kept them using.

This is a proven system that will work if you use the tools.

Since then I have worked with many users- and with few exceptions, enjoyed immediate success, if you are ready to be free from drugs and start to live fully – please work through this book, if you are not ready, believe it will be too hard, and have tried before and failed – work through this book. If you have a loved one, you know is using and want to help, read this book- *to do nothing just guarantees nothing will change for them.*

Read this and be more informed to talk to your children, who are at risk. This book has also been written as a guide to those working with methamphetamine users—as a health professional or therapist, as myself a coach, or as a guide to those doing it themselves. I hope to be explicit enough so that by reading this book, another life is saved. I hope I challenge the clichéd thinking that keeps society in its place and feeling helpless to a scourge that is having a global effect.

This is not an attempt to take on the hypocrisy that exists about whether one drug is more destructive than others that are legal. I'm interested in the use of methamphetamine because of the damage I know it does, and this is my contribution to a better world. When I know I can help, I do.

I do not believe you have to wait for the user to be ready for and want to change. That to me is a misnomer; why expect someone who is not acting rationally to suddenly start making clear and conscious decisions?

I do not believe people have to reach rock bottom, whatever that is. Where else and in what circumstance would we see so much suffering and not intervene, when we know the situation is already out of control? It doesn't have to get any worse to get better. If that was a truism, then everybody who ever used would be dead because surely that must be the worst fate, or "rock bottom."

I do not believe you are powerless over the drug. This belief commits you to a life of remorse, guilt, and craving because if you believe that recovery from methamphetamine is dependent on reason or drive separate from your own, you do not take complete responsibility.

As part of the strategy offered here, you will strengthen your spiritual beliefs and remind yourself of the values you learned as you grew up. You will strengthen the vision you once had for your life and focus your thoughts, behaviors, actions, and habits. Your recovery is up to you, every minute. As part of living a life without using methamphetamine, you will take time to think, meditate, or pray, along with finding new people and activities to replace the old ways.

Sometimes recovery takes just a question from a person concerned enough to ask— remember, most users like to think that there is nothing different or unusual about their behavior. Throughout this book I will be talking to both the user and the concerned friend, and know each of us understand all.

In my experience most methamphetamine users know their life is spiraling out of control, and while they still like what it does, they know they need to stop.

Don't be afraid of a little bit of pain—
pleasure is just the other side.
—JOHN LEGEND, SONGWRITER

SECTION ONE

Chapter One

DRUGS LIMIT YOUR FREEDOM; METHAMPHETAMINE WILL STEAL YOUR SOUL

How did I get here? Somebody pushed me. Somebody must have set me off in this direction, and clusters of other hands must have touched themselves to the controls at different times, for I would not have picked this way for the world.

—JOSEPH HELLER

Life is not always easy for anybody—no matter what the circumstances of your life, you will find others whose life is better or worse than yours. Life is not easy, but it can get better.

I hope this book will challenge your beliefs, explain your apparent lack of choice, and establish new resourceful and strategic behaviors. If you are using, I hope this book will lift your spirits and give you, those that care for you and increasingly, as you free yourself- the people you care for again, better opportunities for the future.

I believe that people always have choices; it may not seem like it, but everything in life comes down to a decision, at every point. So you made a decision and got trapped by drugs, and it's cost you your freedom. You may be in jail or on parole; you may have lost your family, partner, or friends; you may have lost your home, money, career and time—often years. So, make another decision to be free—it may or may not help you get back what you have lost, but it is one way to ensure you won't lose anymore in the same way.

You may be at the mercy of a user, whom you love without question but are afraid of what you see. The person you knew is no more, and you don't know how to help, or maybe you just need to understand what has happened.

There is no stereotypical methamphetamine user- it has breached all boundaries and crossed all convention. There are no rules to who gets trapped into using this drug—*neither is there anyone who needs to stay there.* There is nobody who is irredeemable. There will be some of you who start to read this book simply to look for holes in the simplicity of this system—to admit that changing your addictive behavior can be as simple as a new decision makes it all look too easy. And now for something contentious: many of the apparently well-intentioned helping agencies and drug rehabilitation centers serve to keep the myth alive and keep you using—it keeps them in business.

Whatever excuses you are using now can be turned around in a minute—if you decide to. I do not accept the belief that you will always be a "recovering addict" or crave forever. You will quickly build a new identity and behavior if you follow the structure I will offer you. Ongoing guilt and blame toward yourself does no good. *Letting go of the addict tag takes away your excuses, doesn't it?*

Making recompense to those you have hurt, is one of the means to ease the negative feelings of guilt and regret that can haunt you and keep you using. As you find yourself again you will make right what you can-

Take a look at the misnomer: "it just happened to me." No, it didn't; take responsibility for your actions; you did it. You think a drug that promises nothing but a good time, heightens your mental acuity, and leaves you feeling ecstatic, invincible, blissful, and capable of anything doesn't appeal to all of us as an answer to soothing our emotional, social, and business problems? What makes you think you are so exceptional, different, or important that you can choose to be part of such an insidious behavior?

Maybe you just didn't stop to consider the other side of the story and what the demand you set up means to other innocent people—like the shop keepers that are held up and shot for cash, the home owners that get terrorized or killed when they try to prevent a burglary, the road accidents, and the street violence. Maybe you just don't care about the children that get beaten to death and live in the most horrendous situations.

Methamphetamine is a drug like no other, and it will inevitably steal more from you than it will ever give you.

If you are reading this and think you have no choice it has already done its work.

If you are reading this and don't touch methamphetamine and believe it is hopeless, then it has done its work on you, too. This book is about recovering our society. It will happen when we all take responsibility, and only then, because use is escalating on a global scale.

We are either part of the solution or we are part of the problem

A Hawaiian greeting is to ask "aloha kaua," which translates into "How are we?" Not just you, but how is the relationship with another. It is like asking how is your spirit in conjunction with another?
—THE LITTLE BOOK OF ALOHA

What is most surprising to so many people is how this drug that is sweeping the world crossed all societal boundaries, is known to be so destructive, and is still gathering speed. In spite of so much graphic, lurid information available on the internet to act as a warning, the use of methamphetamine is increasing.

Is it really a symptom of today? This drug promises a shortcut to happiness—euphoria, in fact; an edge in your thinking and all without effort! As a society are we so shortsighted? Have we forgotten everything about being part of the human race?

Methamphetamine is a huge trade, and people, cartels, gangs, and triads are getting rich importing the precursor, the main ingredient from which the drug is manufactured.

I have heard statistics bandied by hospital spokespeople who say up to 75 percent of people attending accident and emergency clinics on weekends are influenced by methamphetamine. There are injuries caused to themselves and others through vehicle accidents, violent robberies, and the crazy, murderous violence that occurs when the user has spent days awake, paranoid and angry and wanting more methamphetamine, for which they will do anything.

Police figures quote the use of methamphetamine as being the fuel behind most of their violent crime. Justice department officials say up to 80 percent of the courts' time involves methamphetamine use.

There are long-lasting social and health problems caused by users of methamphetamine. There is the cost of rehabilitation. I have met people who have gone through expensive and ineffective programs as many as five times, all the time and for years claiming government assistance.

There is the enormous cost to landlords, hoteliers, and local councils who have to risk the lives of fire fighters to clean up methamphetamine laboratories. The environmental impact is savage. Methamphetamine production is dangerous from start to finish and for anybody involved.

Prosecuting users of methamphetamine and the related crimes has placed an enormous burden on justice systems across the world, and the situation is not getting better. While I wrote this, two incidents of interest made the news. A chemist who imported eighty thousand dollars of precursor substance got off scot-free after pleading ignorance about the possible uses of the prepared and packaged goods. A high-profile customs official was busted for his part in a multimillion-dollar ring. It is impossible to extrapolate exact costs, but it is clear that use of methamphetamine on a global scale is increasing because it is seen as so lucrative.

So for you, the user, this is how the story goes, with a few variations of course: First you try it; you like it, so you do it again and again. Soon it consumes you— your time, money, and sense of yourself—and as you lose who you are to this drug, you start to behave like somebody you are not. That's what it does: alter your perceptions, or way of thinking. You then become increasingly paranoid and suspicious. You need more, you get angry, and you need more.

Other people notice the change in you and respond with distrust, disappointment, and annoyance. You lose friends and let others down, you stop caring about things that used to be important, and you do things you never thought you would.

Other users who need to sell to use can pick you out of a crowd, and you sell your body, steal, cheat, and lie at work and to your friends and family. You owe people money—they're smarter than you, and when you can't pay them, they start threatening you and your family. You wonder how this can be happening and then convince yourself it's not, and your need increases.

The stories are not really that different....

Some years ago I was asked to coach two young girls. They were classmates and friends of a child of fifteen who had committed suicide. She had been introduced to methamphetamine by a dealer, an older man she met during her school holidays. As her need to use grew, she started prostituting herself to him for her supply, and to others for his. In four short months of using methamphetamine, her life had degraded to the point where ending it, she believed, was the only option. Her young friends have suffered with the guilt and pain for their friend and for lost innocence—and will do so for years to come.

The supply and demand of methamphetamine means there are babies and children growing up in meth labs with parents who are incapable of giving them care. There is increasingly insidious evidence of brain damage caused by the dangerously toxic chemicals. These kids are living in frequently violent, sexually unsafe, and erratic environments. Other kids at school ostracize them because they smell funny and their parents are scary. A meth lab smells like cat pee: pungent and pervasive. It seeps into clothing, shoes, and skin.

Other kids' parents don't let them play or visit because they know something isn't right, so their ability to socialize is stilted forever, leaving them to grow up seeking the same solutions to dull and avoid the pain in a life they feel they don't fit—because they can't. The nights are disturbed by the illegal activities and parties, where users get together for days at a time. There is nobody able to care for the children, no routines like dinner, bedtimes, school lunches. They are often in filthy surroundings. Frequently other family members have to take over the responsibility for caring for these children because they get deserted by their parents.

Because methamphetamine use creates greater demand in the user, the need to pay for it causes crimes like fraud, robbery, and prostitution. It will leave a legacy for generations to come.

You still think your using doesn't hurt anyone? *If you have a need, it creates a demand, and you are guilty of harm to every child that is living in a meth lab.*

Methamphetamine users cause damage in their lives and in the lives of others because meth users cheat, steal, and lie. There are always stories that start off as lying to yourself, saying things like "This isn't harming anybody. I could give this up anytime I want. I'm just doing it to be social. It's not as if it's heroin…." ad nauseam.

Then the lies progress, you let people down by not being where you said you would be, you lie to avoid suspicion, and suddenly agreements you kept previously to yourself and others become less important. This drug is taking precedence over your life.

Any position you hold in trust is soon at risk. Methamphetamine users are executives who work in Fortune 500 companies, banks, and financial institutions. Nurses and doctors use it; teachers, artists, athletes, company directors, mothers, lawyers, and secretaries get caught up in it. There are no limits; it has crossed all boundaries.

No matter who you are or what you do, if you use methamphetamine, you create a demand, and you are guilty of harm to every child growing up in a methamphetamine lab.

The sooner your behavior becomes your choice, the sooner you are on the way to freedom of choice in all aspects of your life. Stop the supply of this drug—stop your demand.

> *When he reached the new world, Cortez burned his ships—as a result his crew was well motivated.*
> THE HUNT FOR RED OCTOBER

Chapter Two

DAVID: PLEASURE IS JUST THE OTHER SIDE

David came to the office with a concerned family friend. At twenty-five, he was a fit, good-looking young man. He was working in the fast-paced realty market. He lived in an inner-city apartment with his girlfriend, working and playing hard. David had started using methamphetamine about three years previously, it was costing him up to three thousand dollars a week, and he had no intention of giving up.

He had been a bright student, naturally talented at sports, but he had left school before reaching university levels. He had an impatience and anticipation for life urging him; he had always had a sense of adventure. Three years later his erratic behavior was starting to concern those who could still remember him as he had been and now didn't know him at all.

He had always been reliable, kind, and concerned toward his mother and siblings. Over the last six months he had been neglecting his responsibilities, not turning up when he had promised, and borrowing money more and more frequently—until his mother refused to give him money, and then he stopped coming around at all. His mother was finding it too hard to believe there was nothing wrong, so she called a friend and asked for help.

David came to the office one Sunday afternoon with a concerned family friend. He was wired , smoking as she arrived to pick him up. Having been brought up as a polite and responsible young person, David placated his mother's concerns by agreeing to see me, though with no intention of stopping his use.

Here I would like to debunk the misnomer the addicted society perpetuates once again: people don't change unless they want to. This isn't true; they are not acting in a rational, logical way. Why wait for them to want to change while they use a drug that traps them further? Why expect them to make a decision based on rationality and logic?

David was estranged from his father and the father's side of the family. My immediate observation was that it mattered—David was mixed blood. His gender and ethnic identity was connected significantly to the relationship with his extensive family on his father's side. He had suffered his parent's painful divorce as a teenager, a stage of his life where he was learning who he was and where he belonged.

The teenage years are a time of discovery. In an ideal situation a kid gets the opportunity to experiment socially, with parents who guide their adventure, because for kids raised in homes with responsible parents life is adventure and choice. With that, a strong, individual sense of who they are develops, and they believe they are competent and capable and strongly rooted; they know where they belong.

The feeling of confusion and homelessness that comes with irresponsible or incompetent care, however, makes for a shaky foundation. Having an unhappy past does not equate to spending your life in the same comfortable misery. Your choices continue to direct your life. *If you continue to use, you are guaranteed your life at best will stay the same* because it is what you know, but it doesn't have to be this way. Maybe you were one of those with an unfavorable start, but it needn't be an unfavorable finish.

THE PAST DOES NOT EQUAL THE FUTURE

The fact that David had felt he had to turn his back on his father meant the divorce had been acrimonious, and as often happens in divorce, the kids suffered. David had taken on his father's role toward his younger siblings, his own needs treated as unimportant by a mother who unintentionally but unfairly depended on his sacrifice.

David felt he had been burdened with too much responsibility too early, and he was enticed by the nature of methamphetamine. He was a risk taker, impatient, and going places. And here he was today: drug use causing an out of control lifestyle and a cycle of high demand that he was finding impossible to keep up with. David was close to more crime—he had used his mother's credit card and had stolen from her bank account—but David wasn't a bad guy. He had never stolen before, and he loved his mother and family; this is the part where methamphetamine steals your soul.

Users frequently live the illusion that nothing has changed about them, their behavior is stable, and what they are doing doesn't hurt themselves or others. It's not true when taking drugs such as meth, which creates a lifestyle that costs more than the user can afford. They start to take risks, with their own and others' money and possessions. They abuse trust and positions of trust. They start to prostitute and steal. They take up dealing to pay for their own use, and the spiral of harm and deceit escalates for things to stay the same. They hang around people who do the same kind of things—and often worse things. *If you are part of the supply or demand, you are harming others.*

At the very core of drug use (you have noticed I don't use the word addiction, or refer to addicts) is self-centeredness and selfishness. A person who gets himself caught up in the grip of a compulsion that started as a choice and will do anything necessary to continue using, is self-centered to the core.

It may not have started that way. You may have had a strong self-concept or image of yourself that involved caring for others; you may have been a loving and loved father, wife, or friend. However, that must change as you start to trade what you believed yourself to be for something you become. Self-centeredness does not equate to loving oneself excessively. Frequently just the opposite is true: self- loathing is the belief behind selfish, self-absorbed behavior.

David was affronted and quite pissed at me for my approach. I shook his hand to greet him and said, "How long have you been a druggie?" To have a complete stranger say this to him caused him to search for something else in his self-image: his definition of who he was. But you know, I don't think he had any other significant relationship with himself going at the time; he didn't argue, so "druggie" it was. David was lost to himself.

The reason methamphetamine is so insidious is because it affects your brain; methamphetamine is a powerful central nervous system stimulant. The drug works directly on the brain and spinal cord by interfering with normal neurotransmission. Neurotransmitters are chemical substances naturally produced within nerve cells and used to communicate with each other to send messages to influence and regulate our thinking and all other systems throughout the body.

The main neurotransmitter affected by methamphetamine is dopamine. Dopamine is involved with our natural reward system. Feeling good about a job well done, getting pleasure from relationships with our family or social interactions, feeling content that our lives are meaningful and count for something—all these things rely on the transmission of dopamine. Using methamphetamine takes away your body's own ability to feel reward. Suddenly, things that used to have significance have no real meaning anymore.

David was at the point where he no longer had much interest in anything he had previously; he and his girlfriend were existing only to take the drug. They were reliant on more and more meth to satisfy their needs. David had lost a lot of weight, a consequence of the drug and the lack of care for himself (not eating or sleeping properly). He was sallow and pale, and while their relationship was still surviving, they were quickly forgetting how to care for each other, alternating between fighting and a cold distant silence.

She had no interest in coming with David to see me, and David was becoming desperate for money. He was starting to pressure sales, garnering the truth (lying) and not revealing contractual information.

Because of his own high demand, his dealer was keeping him tight. Soon David would be dealing—it was really only a matter of time. Still sound like just recreational use? Not hurting anyone? Not a problem? And you're in control, you can stop anytime? That's the only part that's true—*you can stop anytime, if the pain of using is costing you enough.*

It is hurting you and others, it is a problem and you are losing control. Is that hurting enough yet?

FIND A REASON TO CHANGE

Why would you stop using something that only brings pleasure to you? You won't, and if you do you will continue to crave because you will not have made the essential mind shift that will stop your using easily, instantly, and for good.

A man was walking past a fence and heard a dog yelping. The owner was standing next to the yelping dog. "What's wrong with your dog?" asked the passerby. "He's sitting on a nail," replied the owner. "Why doesn't he get off?" "Because it's not hurting him enough."

THOUGHTS ARE REAL, EVERYTHING BEGINS WITH A THOUGHT

What are you thinking?

Often with methamphetamine users, when their behavior gets so crazy and erratic, people who care intervene—and often are scared or warded off, so they leave it be. When the user is high, they often feel euphoric and invincible. It is easy to believe and hope for the best, so you leave them alone. Then the anxiety, anger, or depression sets in, and you leave them alone because they don't want your help. You are afraid to say anything—it's not your business to interfere, you don't have any proof, it's their choice—like I did with my friend, who died.

David had a few sores on his face and a slight twitch above his eye, signs of extensive use. He also had a lot of bravado; he was going to keep up the bluff. He had smoked less than an hour before, and comedown is rapid. Users get together and go for days—they want it to last, and nothing else takes precedence, which is why child abuse is so related to meth users and their lifestyle. When children are around, they are subject to cruelty, sexual abuse, and neglect. Are you looking a little selfish now?

If you are part of the supply and demand of this filthy drug, you are guilty of all the above!

In a study, laboratory rats pressed levers to release methamphetamine into their blood stream rather than eat, mate, or satisfy other natural drives. The animals died of starvation while giving themselves methamphetamine even though food was available. Thank goodness that as humans we have the ability to reason, objectify, and visualize. If we didn't, we might also be hapless victims, like lab rats.

All so-called addictive drugs have two things in common: they produce an initial pleasurable effect, followed by a rebound unpleasant effect. Methamphetamine, through its stimulant effects, produces a positive feeling but later leaves a person feeling depressed, and as use progresses, depression occurs more and more frequently. This is because it suppresses the normal production of dopamine, creating a chemical imbalance. The user physically demands more of the drug to return to normal. This pleasure/tension cycle leads to loss of control over the drug.

The higher you go, the harder you fall.
—GRANDPARENTS' WISDOM

Methamphetamine short-circuits a person's survival system by artificially stimulating the reward center, or pleasure areas in the brain. This leads to increased confidence in meth and less confidence in the normal rewards of life. This happens on a physical, chemical level at first, then it affects the user psychologically. The result is decreased interest in other aspects of life while reliance and interest in meth increases. However it starts, it ends its hold only one way:- *you decide to be free first*—after all, you decided to start using.

Methamphetamine causes a variety of mental, physical, and social problems to the user and to their family. Although not as expensive as heroin and cocaine, as use increases, it causes financial problems, creates stress, changes behavior, and exacerbates relationship difficulties. This highlights the fact that people don't get the help they need soon enough—*the most commonly reported reason for methamphetamine users to enter treatment is trouble with the law.* These legal problems include aggressive or bizarre behaviors that prompt other people to call police. Other reasons for intervention include charges of burglary and theft. They include mental or emotional problems and situations at work that often involve fraud, with criminal charges often following.

DRUGS DO NOT LOVE YOU

Drug use that is extensive and out of control rarely has a happy ending because in order to maintain your use, something (if not everything) about you will have to be sacrificed. Gaining the love and respect back for yourself and others is paramount, even if at first you don't think you deserve it. Maybe you will have to learn what it is to love yourself again, or perhaps truly learn for the first time.

The Creator had a secret he wanted to share with the humans- but he didn't want them to discover it until they were ready, the secret? That we create our own reality.

Soon a mighty eagle appeared and said to the Creator- "Give me the secret – I will catch the wind, and fly with it to the highest cliff, and put it in the craggiest spot I can find". "No" said the Creator, "The humans will go there and find it",

The dolphin said "Give me the secret- I will swim to the deepest part of the ocean, and leave it there"- "No" said the Creator,

"They will go there and find it"

The bear suggested he take it to the darkest cave he knew of, but again the Creator refused.

Then Grandmother Mole, who lives in the bowels of Mother Earth, and is blind, she sees only with spiritual eyes said "Put it inside them" and the Creator said, "It is done."

Chapter Three

A Reason to Change

The first years of our lives dictate the way we think, perceive, and relate. If you must, this book will show you how to relearn, to start again the way you want it to be, to become more of the person you were meant to be. Many readers will at this point and decide to use their unhealthy and unhappy beginnings as the reason for poor choices, but if all it takes is an attitude change, why continue to perpetuate the myth that life will always be that way?

Enough to make you think it's all too hard? It is if you don't know what you want instead. The hardest part is what to do with a life you reclaim and start to live consciously. There is so much more once this spell is broken. And that is not as impossible as you may feel. *The first thing to do is acknowledge that you are responsible for your life today*

The good news is the fight to stop this drug destroying any more of your life can be decided now- this book is about being free, not staying trapped. So, the first part is easy-new behaviors can be adapted easily- if you decide to be willing enough, and your loathing turns itself onto the drug that has you in its grip; one that is distorting your mind, behavior and actions.

FIND A REASON TO CHANGE.

David was a real nice guy, and he was really screwing up. The first questions I ask a meth user are about what his life looks like today. It's a self-report; it is entirely up to the client to decide, and it is based on his experience and expectations.

David was a little shocked at where he saw himself in his life. Maybe it was the first truly honest inventory he had taken for a long while. Part of the attraction to the drug was David's desire for more, quicker and faster; he liked what the drug had first promised. He was confident and strong—in the beginning, anyway. David had always enjoyed good things: travel had been something he enjoyed, and he used to play sports every weekend. Now he took drugs.

David was asked what he had learned to expect and what he understood about the significant areas of his life. His primary focus went to family and friends: he had disappointed people, most important his mother, and of course the distance between them had grown. Sometimes all it takes is the first step; just by getting together, the past can be put behind. Sometimes that is not possible because the damage has been too extensive, and building trust back over time, and by trial, is what it will take.

In some circumstances there is a benefit to you remaining hopeless because you can be blamed for all the conflict, you can take the blame for failed relationship and bad business decisions and every financial disaster ever committed, and you can remind yourself and be reminded daily that it is your fault.

You can't change what you have done - just stop doing it.

The other person or people involved can feel guiltless, and while often they are implicated heavily, they can make themselves look better and more virtuous than you. This is most often your closest family or friends.

You may be in an environment where this is the only way. You have been bought up in a home where using drugs are okay and methamphetamine is acceptable. You will have to go against all you knew and the family life you lived in. Somebody has to break the cycle, and it has to be you.

Sometimes, there has been just too much damage done by you, toward others who were an innocent party. If you can't do anything to make it better right now, then breaking all relationships until you stop using is imperative. You are better off free to start a new life and gain a sense of self-respect back.

Financially, David had nothing left. He had previously owned an expensive, late-model car. He didn't have it anymore, and they were behind in their rent in the apartment they had expected to own by now. David had always had a lot of pride, and this was humiliating for him. He was barely managing to eat and was in debt. Surprisingly, as we spoke and he got a bit clearer, his biggest disappointment was the fact he wanted to marry Ally one day, and this wasn't the way it would happen.

This acted as leverage and the reason for him to do something different.

He was starting to consider the cost of the lifestyle he was living now. For a future thinker like David, somebody with the gift of vision, his life was quite pathetic. David had grown up with expectations, dreams of things he would accomplish. He had an entrepreneurial spirit and was hard working, but for what? That day, for the first time in a long time, David had looked at his life for what it was, as it was.

He hadn't cared up until now—the euphoria from the smoke he had just had was well over. He was starting to become agitated; it was very obvious he wanted to get out as soon as he could to have another smoke. Remember, David had no intention of giving up.

We started talking about his family. He hadn't seen his father, uncles, or cousins for five years. I asked whether David would consider contacting his father. While the idea wasn't met with complete disinterest, it really wasn't in his plan for today. David seemed vulnerable, a little pensive and subdued, still a kid.

The next part I used as leverage was his vanity. He was dressed well and expensively, but it was definitely last year's style. He had the slightest mark on his face, so I asked him how often he got open sores. The last hour had been a little surprising for David, having a stranger exposing him. Then I mentioned his facial twitch, which really seemed to upset him.

We talked more about David's life as it was, with no more excuses. There was no doubt that if David kept doing what he was doing, his life was only going to get worse. Over this hour David had started a transformation in his thinking, against his own wishes. By the time he left, he would be choosing and capable of a life of freedom. That's really how simple it is: *make a decision, make a change.*

There is little to be gained from agonizing over the past when you can make a decision for immediate change, because the past is now gone. You can't change that.

David's dad had a concrete laying business, just the opportunity for David to get out of the environment he was in and work hard physically to detoxify his body, as well as accomplishing the obvious: reunite a father and son and end the pain their separation was costing them. He agreed by this time he needed to change his lifestyle. The fact his girlfriend had no interest in coming here with him made it clear that love loses its meaning pretty quickly. Although they had been together from the beginning (they met as seventeen year olds) and had been very happy, the meth use took hold. A drug like meth is like having a love affair with a third person in a relationship—one that takes precedence.

If you were to ask, they would still say they were happy, but their plans for the future were further away. They were living from one day to the next, going through the motions until they were sure they would have a supply of the drug for that session, that day. Their work circumstances exacerbated the situation: they each made generous commissions, and with nothing in between, neither had a stable income. When they had earned, the drug was plentiful and they would binge, spending thousands of dollars over a week. But if they hadn't made sales, they couldn't buy, and in understanding how the need to use more to get the same high escalates, they got desperate. It was already the reason they had stolen from their parents, who trusted them. It was a matter of time before one or the other turned to dealing in order to supply themselves.

As David recounted his story, he was increasingly agitated. He started fidgeting, his legs moved restlessly, and he started sweating. If you have ever been in the same room as a meth user who is detoxifying, you will not need me to tell you that they stink!

Ally chose to stay doing what she was doing. For David to change his life, he had to leave her, the people he was spending time with who did drugs, and the environment he was living in, and go to his father's house to start to live free.

Chapter Four

You Forget Who You Are

When asked about his values and honesty and success, David's realization was immediate: he used to live by them, but now he didn't. Values help define us and act as our most important motivation or driver. We all have a set of values that must not be contrived- everybody has something that must not be violated. Methamphetamine makes you forget what they are as you start to forget who how you are. .

I asked a user who was also a meth cook why he had started manufacturing methamphetamine. He first got involved in supply because he saw what was being charged in the street and how the quality varied. He decided that being a good friend meant providing safe drugs, without the cost being too high, so in his mind he justified his criminal behavior by twisting reality this way. Kindness and fairness were two important factors in his decision to start making methamphetamine! By discovering the values he held up, I could relate to him a few horror stories about the cruelty, neglect, and violence that is such a trademark symptom of meth psychosis.

Is it fair when babies and children get taken to hospital with multiple wounds like broken bones, severe bruising, and infected sores caused by cigarette burns and beatings from adults who are sleep deprived and paranoid from using meth, which proves to be the impetus behind the evil? *If you are part of the supply and demand, you are responsible.*

David called his father from my office at the point he realized things could no longer go on as they had and he needed to make a change for his life. He made a decision to stop using methamphetamine and start living again with no more excuses, lies, or false promises. People do the best with what they know, and when they know more, they often do better. At this point for David, there was no turning back.

> Before a butterfly can emerge from it's chrysalis, it has to go through a lot of struggling. Each time it lunges out to escape, acids are being removed from its wings. If someone were to come along and break the chrysalis open for it, then the butterfly would die from those acids— the struggle is necessary. When the struggle is over, the butterfly emerges to share its beauty. As humans, are we any different? There are times we need to struggle to become all we can be. We need to struggle with the acids that make up sadness, fear, and anger, and emerge...

David left the office that day, went to his apartment for all he could throw in a bag, and walked out. Ally stayed and partied on with his friends, who did not believe it could or would be so easy.

David had made his mind up. He knew what to do and had a place to go. His friends had neither, or so they thought...

DAVID'S STORY

I felt like shit, telling my girlfriend about leaving, but I didn't want anything to do with drugs anymore. That promise I made to myself was the first I had kept for nearly three years. After getting my stuff, I went to my dad's. He lived a little bit out of the city. When I talked to him on the phone, I didn't tell him much, but he knew it must have been pretty bad for me to need to live with him.

Making the choice was easy. In the office I had taken a good look at my life for the first time—where I was and where I was going. I decided that whatever happened, whatever I was in for couldn't be anywhere as bad as where I was. I got straight into working. The next morning I went to work as a laborer, working at my dad's concrete company.

I ached; I think it was because I had to work hard, and also detox can leave your joints a bit stiff. I just drank plenty of water. The first few days were hard. I missed Ally, but I had to put all my attention on getting my life back on track. I got up early, had breakfast, worked all day, and came home, and for the first time in ages,

I started sleeping. I can't even remember dreaming—I was used to staying up all night, and sometimes my user friends and I would go three days before needing to crash. You get a little crazy, but I never did anything too bad. Once we smashed up a bit of furniture—being stupid, no reason.

I cried because of the things I had said and done, like stealing from my mum. I didn't care who I hurt, I just did whatever I could to get the money. That helped, and it was strange to feel again because I hadn't felt emotions for a long time.

Actually, I did do other stupid shit, like driving dangerously, and risking other people's lives didn't even come into consideration. I let people down and wasted a ton of money, but I knew I had to look forward and not worry about things I couldn't change and make up for what I could-

I met up with my cousins and my uncles, and I saw a couple of relly's (relatives) going the same way I had. They reminded me of what I didn't want any longer. And the best part was how by the first weekend Ally and two of my mates came and lived with my dad as well. They got chucked out of where they were living, and at first I don't think they thought I was serious, but my dad was, and he let them stay if they worked, like I did. Ally got a new job and went out to work every day. We all hung out together, we weren't allowed to speak about using, and we had to stay around the house. All of us are drug free now. Ally and I got married, and we have our first child due soon.

I have a good job and a nice car, and we moved into our first home six weeks ago. I would not be capable of any of this if I was still using, and I didn't know that at the time.

My mum trusts me most of the time now. It's been okay for a while—not at first though. I think she blamed herself. She was angry I went to my dad's to get better, and she didn't know what I'd been up to; she said she had lost me for a couple of years. I promised never to hurt her or myself like that again. I understand her own life wasn't easy. She is not responsible for what I did in my life—I am and always will be.

When Christina rang me about the book it was the first time in two years- I dropped the phone- it was a shock to imagine that person she is writing about was

me. My Grandmother had died that morning and I was driving to see her body-
it was kind of like a message, it's hard to accept that meth had me the way it did-
and now it's even harder to see what keeps people using it. It's not as if it felt great
all the time I was using- and sometimes it was. But nowhere near getting back to
enjoying all the things and times I used to.

DAVID'S STRATEGIES

- Take a look at what it's costing you- on all levels, physical, emotional, spiritual and mental. When I had to admit I had become a liar and thief, I was hurting the people in my life I had least reason to. That was the straight talking reality check I needed. My body was wrecked, I wasn't playing sport anymore, my face was starting to look scabby, I was always looking for money to spend on drugs, was way out of touch with anyone who didn't use, facing this meant I only had one choice and one decision to make after that.

- Get out of the environment where you use drugs, and the people who use with you. Only hang with people that will talk you up, and believe it is easy to stop. My Dad didn't want to know all the bad shit- just how we could make it good- he wouldn't have put up with any trouble either, getting better wasn't an option, it was how it was going to be. I know not everyone has that kind of support- but staying in the same place means nothing will change. I made the first step- and my friends followed me-

- Just get back to doing smart stuff, like good habits and routines, eating and sleeping, playing sport, get around good people, be aware of what you do when you're stressed up (so you can do something other than drugs) think good things, and make up for the bad things you have done- forgive yourself and help others. I know I'm lucky.

- Make plans, set goals, they might change but that's ok, it's who you become on the way that's important Setting goals mean you start habits again to get you there- and you feel good as you start to achieve them. Keep your agreements- be on time, and reliable –and you will start to build trust back again-

- Never make any more excuses- that shit is bad- there is no reason or excuse I could use that would ever be worth that again. Tell the truth, always, and if I can help by telling somebody else how easy it was to get off it – I will.

- Start dreaming again- make your life the way you want it be. I have never touched meth again since that day, I could have made all the excuses in the world and kept doing it- and been deeper in trouble.

Chapter Five

PAUL: I JUST WANTED TO STOP THIS, AND DIDN'T WANT IT TO STOP

If you ever wake up without a problem, you better get down on your knees and pray for one, because otherwise you just died.
—NORMAN VINCENT PEALE

Paul was well built and had a great smile and an easy personality. He started using methamphetamine as a body builder when he was competing for titles, which put the pressure on him to do better—meth makes you angry and charged enough to lift weights that aren't possible without it. Students sometimes begin using meth because of the initial heightened physical and mental performance the drug produces. Blue-collar and service workers like chefs and truck drivers may use the drug to work extra shifts; hence the trend of drug testing in many industries now. Women often begin using meth to lose weight. Others use meth recreationally to stay energized at rave parties, or to be part of the crowd they hang out with.

And that's how it started for Paul, some eight years before. It wasn't the first drug he had ever used. Smoking dope then using ecstasy, cocaine, and speed had been pretty constant since his very early teens.

He won the competition, and it was during training for a second title that Paul suffered a heart attack—at twenty-six. He had put so much stress on his body through using speed that it nearly killed him. He had extensive, life-saving surgery and spent two months in the intensive care unit. It didn't stop him. He had just met Teresa. She was there constantly during his hospital stay while he recovered, and while she still had no idea of the extent of his use, he stopped smoking methamphetamine. They were in love.

Because it can be made easily and a lab can be set up in an hour, meth is less expensive and more accessible than cocaine, and users sometimes pretend that methamphetamine is not really a drug. Methamphetamine is made up of cold and asthma medications containing ephedrine or pseudoephedrine. These ingredients are known as precursors and are substances that in nature might be inactive, but when mixed together the result is a new product.

Methamphetamine starts with an inactive or marginally inactive compound (ephedrine or pseudoephedrine). Other chemicals are added to produce the drug: red phosphorous, hydrochloric acid, drain cleaner, battery acid, lye, lantern fuel, and antifreeze are among the ingredients most commonly used. Yum!

Methamphetamine can be smoked, snorted, injected intravenously, or ingested orally. The drug alters moods in different ways, depending on how it is taken. I refer mostly to smoking meth unless the details are important. Immediately after smoking or intravenous injection, the user experiences an intense rush or flash that lasts only a few minutes and is described as extremely pleasurable. Smoking or injecting produces effects fastest, within five to ten seconds. Snorting or ingesting orally produces euphoria—a high but not an intense rush. It is often never the same intensity again, which gets users seeking it again and again.

Meth stimulates the central nervous system, with effects lasting anywhere from four to twenty-four hours. Methamphetamine use can not only modify behavior in an acute state, but after being taken it for a long time, the drug literally changes the brain in fundamental and long-lasting ways. It kills by causing heart failure, brain damage, or strokes, and it can induce extreme, acute psychiatric and psychological symptoms that may lead to suicide or murder.

It affects the central nervous system that commands your body's responses. Even small amounts of methamphetamine can produce euphoria, increased alertness, paranoia, decreased appetite, and increased physical activity. Other central nervous system effects include writhing, jerky, or flailing movements; irritability; extreme nervousness; insomnia; confusion; tremors; anxiety; aggression; incessant talking; hyperthermia; and convulsions. Your body is in a state of high excitement at first, then that excitement becomes anxiety.

Sounds like real fun.

About three months out of hospital, Paul started using again, more regularly than before. At this point Teresa seemed to accept his use but the extent to which he used, the connections he had, and how intertwined their lives would be with other users was unknown to her. Their friends were gang members who manufactured and sold the drug on a large scale, the people he supplied and sold to, and as time went by the more desperate friends whose lives and families fell apart, with nowhere else to go. His use escalated rapidly.

Paul had been a hard worker. He had established a business of which he was once proud, but over the last four years he had drained all its cash resources to support the drug that was taking over every thought, every day.

His day began with his first smoke. He smoked as he drove to work, then frequently throughout the day. His mates dropped in regularly throughout the day and night. He wasn't using drugs; they were using him.

Paul and Teresa were in love, or so they said. He would tell you he got more involved in selling to pay for the wedding. She would say she only agreed because they had a wedding to pay for.

Paul saw no reason to stop using meth. He took stock of his life and saw friends suffering from using, but it still had not deterred him. They married, and at the wedding reception, after most of the guests had gone, he smoked methamphetamine with his mates. For Teresa that was unforgivable.

They went overseas on their honeymoon, and maybe this was where he discovered he had a growing need for the drug. He couldn't get any, and their idyllic holiday became a massive comedown. He was in turn agitated then exhausted, and he spent most of their time on the honeymoon asleep all day and awake all night, sweating and short-tempered, watching TV, unable to laugh or have sex, with no inclination to go out.

Very early into the marriage they could no longer keep up the pretense they had fallen into. He was using a lot, practically all the time. She was using methamphetamine to keep her weight down, and drinking alcohol to forget.

All his friends used. He went to work every day and saw no harm in what he was doing. He was emotionally unavailable to love either his wife or himself. She had no means to appeal to him; he just didn't feel anything other than the love affair he was desperate to consummate as much and as often as possible-with methamphetamine.

They were both lonely when they were together, frozen and detached. Methamphetamine has that effect: you think you're being charismatic, but really you're not.

At the same time Teresa's dependence on alcohol was getting out of control, she was angry, but still didn't say why. At the point Paul approached me, they had separated, and it was his business that he wanted coaching in. Paul was more than happy to keep on using; he saw absolutely no harm in what he was doing.

Paul was articulate, intelligent, a nice guy. I had met his wife first, socially, and for a while had no idea what they were hiding and thought her unhappiness was due to work stress, inability to conceive, and the demands of daily living. They had both used cocaine and taken party drugs regularly, and each took a liberal stance: they weren't harming anyone else. Then he started replacing that with methamphetamine.

Teresa never disclosed their secret, ever. I had my suspicions, but because of her shame and the pain of coming second, Teresa would avoid any question of help. It took me a while to put the clues together, and by the time I did, Paul was in trouble; she left him, without saying why.

PAUL'S STORY

I had been smoking methamphetamine for almost five years, and I had been using more and more. But I was never aggressive, always quite mellow, just sharper—at least, (that's what I thought. When I think back, though, I had everything going my way; I had a good cash business and worked a bit extra on weekends—that was easy. When it got too expensive, I started supplying. I started turning over some good money. I thought that when I left Teresa things would level out and I would reduce my use a little.

The marriage stressed me out, and in all honesty I did believe there was no noticeable change in me. In retrospect, I see it now. I really did not care about anything over the last two years but smoking meth. My mates came into work, and we'd smoke during and after, and after Teresa and I split up, it got worse, it was costing me more and more, so I did longer hours and justified using it that way.

I realize, again in retrospect, how little empathy or interest I showed anybody in my life at the time, especially my wife. I avoided my parents (they didn't know what was happening) and stopped talking to my brother and sister and their spouses. I can't believe I didn't stop after my heart attack. I just didn't care and couldn't feel. At the same time I kept telling myself I could stop any time I wanted to. I think I know what it meant to lose your soul for a time—women would come into my shop, and if I was high(as I wrote this I made a comment to myself about always being smashed—not if, always) I'd cheat on my wife, seeing them as trophies, conquests, a bit of fun. Not something I ever thought I would do, and I would never do now. I really didn't see them as anything animate or real at all. I certainly had lost respect.

It was not long after my marriage fell apart that I got invited to do a workshop on planning for the business. My business was in trouble by now; I had sold half the shares to a guy who didn't like what I was doing and put up with it anyway. However, the content had a far greater scope, and we were asked to take a look at our whole life. I had just ended my marriage and started a relationship with a girl who cooked methamphetamine. She lived in a warehouse, and I was living there most of the time.

I would arrive to the seminar late, smoked up, and as the morning progressed, I start sweating, waiting till I got a break to go downstairs into the car park and have a smoke—maybe four times a day. I still don't know when they (the others at the workshop) guessed, but I started feeling more and more of a fraud, started to see what this was costing me. I wanted out from facing this truth, but there were still two weekends to go.

That afternoon we started talking about how we form our value systems, what we stand for, and how we reflect them. We got onto the topic of drugs and the argument about personal freedom as opposed to the rights and safety of others. I listened more than talked. It just didn't make any sense any longer, and I had run out of arguments. I just wanted to stop this, and I didn't want it to stop.

The next weekend by midmorning of the first day, when I hadn't showed up, Christina rang me. I had something more important to do: the evening before I had decided to stop using meth, moved out of the warehouse, turned up the next day and spoke openly about my choice. I was offered absolute support, and it all seemed too easy. I changed the routine I was in, told my business partner so he knew what to look out for, and did what I could to start living so that I could be proud of myself again. I had to make adjustments to every part of my life.

Being seen as a bad guy didn't fit with me. I've always been known as someone who would help a friend, who was relaxed and happy—and I was, but my relationship with Teresa and my marriage didn't stand a chance the way I had treated her.

In fact I was anything but those things to her. So honesty was the best first policy. I had just barely hung onto my business and considered myself pretty lucky, but I took a serious look at what this drug was costing me. It was starting to look like too much

PAUL'S STRATEGIES

- One of the significant exercises I did was make a list about who I was, what I meant to others, and what was good about me. That was important.

- I stopped seeing the friends who I took drugs with. I had to, and they had to stay away—at first. Part of that also included taking a solid look at how I was spending my time at work. I started following a daily schedule, starting jobs when I said I would, attending meetings I had agreed to, being generally reliable. The business improved because the guys I employed started to show me a little bit of respect again; they told me it was because I started making sense. I didn't ever think I hadn't.

- I did what I could to be as fair as I could in the divorce settlement. I was sorry for what I had done during our marriage and apologized to Teresa's family. I was there when she needed me to talk through the things we hadn't before. I felt like I was doing my best, so I felt better. There are things that will never be the same. I had to rebuild, little by little, trust and respect for myself.

- I started reading again.

- I spent time establishing a relationship with my parents; they still don't know what happened and have said things seem back to normal. I wondered about telling them but decided all that mattered now was we were okay again.

- I watched my diet. I never really drank alcohol, and I exercised.

- I had my nephew and niece to visit more regularly.

- I worked as hard as I could. It was tempting to use again, but the reason I didn't was the realization that meth has caused so much pain. It was also about this time there were some pretty awful things going on in the news, people doing crazy, psycho things. I didn't see any fun in that, and I couldn't excuse myself anymore.

- I wanted to smoke daily, often—the craving was for the good times, friends I had known for years. So by deciding I wanted something different for me, they weren't the people I needed around me for the moment. Since I have stopped, so have a couple of acquaintances; they came to me for support, and I helped them.

- Specifically, the best strategy was changing the picture in my mind about meth and seeing it for what it was and the damage I had done to myself and others.

Paul's strategy here was to link pain to continued using. The pain must be greater than any pleasure you can still imagine, and if you feel weak, focus, enlarge, and elaborate on that pain of continuing using. Then build a picture of how you see yourself after you get through this: free and well and being decent to the people who need you to be there for them again.

What action will you take? If you cave in and start using again, just this once, it means more than that—you have once more given up on yourself, your promises, your integrity, and the right to be trusted. *Don't give up—it won't always be this tough.*

Take these steps, make a deal with yourself by resisting right now, just this moment, hour, morning, afternoon, evening. Taking action right now will determine your life one way or another.

No surprises, are there?

Thoughts become real. Fill your head with new, resourceful thoughts, behaviors, stories, and references.

Two years later, I caught up with Paul. His business is prospering, and he is happy and engaged to a woman with whom he is deeply in love. They are about to travel across Europe, something he never dreamed he would do. For such a long time while he used, most of his late teens and twenties, all he thought about was methamphetamine: his supply, his use, and how he could pay for it.

He is completely drug free now and could not be convinced under any circumstance to ever touch anything again, especially methamphetamine. He has helped friends by giving them a job while they stop. He is free.

Chapter Six

METHAMPHETAMINE DOES NOT LOVE YOU

By the time Jackie's partner sought help for himself, Jackie was simply skin and bones. She was emaciated; her skin had an unhealthy, almost translucent look, full of scabs she picked constantly. By this time they had been using for two years, her kidneys were failing, her face twitched, her hair was thin and falling out in clumps, and she was delusional, paranoid, and invincible.

Her partner came to me because their business was failing. It was too late to redeem it, and no point in trying, either—Jackie had stolen money and written checks that had caused outrageous debt. Her elderly parents had guaranteed the loan, and they lost their home.

I believe at this stage she should have been restrained without her consent and treated in an institution; by this time she was very sick and destructive. When you believe it is helpless, it becomes that way. I think the people closest to her gave up in their efforts because they had been told there was nothing they could do.

Still, she didn't care. When their relationship was ended by my client, Jackie started living in her car, stealing and lying. She had sold everything of any value, so she started work as a prostitute. Even though the stress of watching their daughter choosing to kill herself devastated her parents, they tried to keep loving her, but meth made Jackie seek nothing from anyone else.

Jackie's lungs were at the point of collapsing from so much toxic meth smoke, and a friend who was a nurse and a user herself showed Jackie how to inject one hundred dollars a time into her arms, legs, backside, between her toes—anywhere she could put a needle. Her frail, tiny, emaciated arms became a welt of weeping sores, and when she couldn't get meth to inject, she used water—she was used to injecting. It soothed her. She cut herself, and she also burned her arms and legs with cigarettes to distract herself and cause the pain that had become so familiar.

After three years of using methamphetamine, a bright, vibrant and talented daughter, business owner, lover, friend, and sister was found slumped over her steering wheel, the windows up, engine running, and a hose running from the exhaust pipe to the inside of her car. She survived this anyway....

Jackie decided she would start manufacturing and dealing, so she made one thousand dollars worth of meth. When she went to the gang headquarters to sell it to her arranged buyers, they beat her up, stole it from her, and threw her out -

A year later, at thirty-four, Jackie's use of meth caused permanent damage to the blood vessels in her brain, and she suffered a stroke. Self-inflicted? *Not if you were the ones smoking with her, not if you sold it to her. If you are sharing drugs with someone like Jackie, you're as responsible as she is for her imminent death,* unless of course you want to argue that she was not in her right mind— that's true, but it's no defense for your actions.

If you know someone like Jackie, make her get help. It is not too late, hopeless, or impossible. If this sounds like you, and you don't make a choice to stop, you could end up like Jackie, and it could get worse. I caught you then, so who cares? Probably more people than you know, and if you can't think of anybody who cares, that's the proof that taking a drug like methamphetamine doesn't make you charismatic, vibrant, and powerful. Start by taking a realistic new look at your life, and change it, because you've been looking in the wrong places.

What about Jackie's partner, my client? He went bankrupt, as his part of the business they were in together collapsing.

The good news is he stopped using immediately without any angst, and while he had no time off work, he is completely free of methamphetamine. Three years later he is still paying off the creditors through the courts. The pain he feels is about the regret of losing Jackie when it could have been so different.

There is the gap in his now-adult children's lives. He wasn't there for them while they grew up, and he wanted to talk to him about boys and girls, and whether they should do drugs, what they wanted from life, and did one need to be good at math to become a quantity surveyor—he wanted to give them the guidance and wisdom a parent can provide. He wasn't there for that. He's okay now, though, and is doing his best. He's the first and most vehement to tell you never, ever touch the filthy, lying drug, it's not worth it.

One thing is for sure: using drugs and alcohol is
not a path to one's inner-most feelings,
*"otherwise people wouldn't smash empty beer cans against their skulls
and stick their fingers in a fire to see if they can feel anything"*
—GREG BEHRENDT AND LIZ TUCCILLO

The reason people take drugs is to replicate or alter their reality. The reason people don't take drugs is because they don't need to.

The way meth works is to interfere with the way we think when we feel good. It steals our ability to achieve the very thing we are looking for, and it will eventually leave you ashamed, bereft and still searching.

METHAMPHETAMINE DOES NOT LOVE YOU.

The cardiovascular side effects of using the drug are chest pains and hypertension, which can result in cardiovascular collapse and death. In addition, methamphetamine causes accelerated heartbeat, elevated blood pressure, and irreversible damage to blood vessels in the brain.

Other physical effects include pupil dilation, respiratory disorders, dizziness, tooth grinding, impaired speech, dry or itchy skin, loss of appetite, acne, sores, numbness, and sweating.

The psychological effects of prolonged methamphetamine use can resemble those of schizophrenia: anger, panic, paranoia, auditory and visual hallucinations, and repetitive behavior patterns. It leaves users with delusions of parasites or insects on the skin, which they sometimes try to cut out.

Methamphetamine-induced paranoia can result in homicidal or suicidal thoughts. Are you having fun yet?

Other long-term effects can result in fatal kidney and lung disorders, brain damage, liver damage, blood clots, chronic depression, hallucinations, violent and aggressive behavior, malnutrition, disturbed personality development, and deficient immune system. The user may exhibit anxiousness; nervousness; incessant talking, extreme moodiness, irritability, purposeless, repetitious behavior (such as picking at skin or pulling out hair), sleep disturbances, false sense of confidence and power; aggressive or violent behavior; disinterest in previously enjoyed activities, and severe depression (which increases the risk of suicide). Because stimulants affect the body's cardiovascular and temperature-regulating systems, physical exertion increases the hazards of meth use.

In that time I was self-employed, made some good coin, bought two new vehicles, broke my mum's heart some more—then I showed up at her house. I was ashamed and sick. Why didn't I just get help? Because a big part of me has always been self-destructive, and methamphetamine let me be the one to hurt myself.

—UNKNOWN USER

Chapter Seven
INTENTION IS NEVER ENOUGH

Methamphetamine is a class A illicit drug and is made in laboratories often set up in garages, motels, or rental properties. Methamphetamine has no standardized dose or formula. This increases the risk of using because the potency, effects, and dangers of the drug change every time you use.

How much of the drug can cause an overdose? A toxic reaction (or overdose) can occur at relatively low levels: fifty milligrams of pure drug for a nontolerant user. Metabolic rates vary from person to person, and the strength of the illegal form of the drug varies from batch to batch, so there is no way of stating what a "safe" level of use is.

I believe it is completely unjust that our society pays the cost of hospitalization and rehabilitation when illegal drug use is proven. Make the user pay. *If it takes the rest of their lives, so be it—at least they have a "rest" to their life!*

Babies born to methamphetamine users can suffer birth defects and low birth weight, have tremors, cry excessively, develop attention deficit disorder, and have behavioral disorders. Having such a distressed start to life and then experiencing parents who are trapped in use virtually guarantee child abuse and neglect, and so it continues. If there are babies or children you know with family members who are using, take them away before they get hurt—it doesn't always show, and they will get hurt. *Take them away until their parents stop using—no exceptions.*

The use of methamphetamine has offered a hard reality in New Zealand. Alongside the escalating use that has been observed so too has violent crime and murder . Where previously we did not see such horrific crime, we do now and attribution to methamphetamine use is. To our shame, we have horrific stories before the courts, with meth use being prevalent.

Remember, meth users frequently go on binges together, and while so far I haven't worked with any of the people involved in the following incidences while smoking and suffering bizarre hallucinations, people in groups do things that on their own they wouldn't. This leads to the horrific stories that fill the press and television In the New Zealand press we hear of children being beaten to death, put in clothes dryers and then hung out on the washing line, used as balls and kicked around rooms by groups of binging adults, their parents included.

In one infamous case, while in a paranoid violent rage a user took a machete and severed the arms of his girlfriend.

In another high profile case, twin babies were beaten to death, the accused escaping conviction because the twelve adults present during the babies short tortured lives had their wits about them enough to stymie police investigation.

In New Zealand the gangs who command the supply and demand of methamphetamine have stopped the use of the drug amongst their own-because it does so much damage. If you still think there can be such a thing as recreational use-think again.

When does someone else's right to break the law and endanger society take precedence? It doesn't.

I met Jonathon's mother at a party. She started talking to me about her son, a hopeless addict. He was such a nice boy when he was little, but for the last seven years his life had taken a bad turn. He had been taking drugs since smoking marijuana at sixteen; at eighteen he started using heroin, overdosed while using it, then got HIV from sex with a girl who had caught it from sharing needles.

While he said he preferred heroin, meth was cheaper and very available. His mother was dying of cancer, and her obvious only wish was that when she died, her son would be free of drugs. He had just been thrown out of a residential drug rehab program, again—this was his fifth admission. At this point he was reckless; he felt he had nothing to go on for.

Jonathon had been brought up by his mother. She had enjoyed a very successful career, but now, in her early fifties, cancer had chosen her fate. It was easy to understand why Jonathon no longer had the impetus to stop using: his drug sent him into oblivion, which meant most of the time he thought he was able to forget the reality of his life. But drug taking is reality; there is nothing unreal about it, and it only makes things worse, not better.

Jonathon believed he had outwitted years of psychiatrists, counselors, and extended family advice, threats, and cajoling. Jonathon was a bright person who was more than content to continue using. The night he left rehab, he injected meth. A week later he came into my office for his first session. He was a good looking man—twenty-nine, well dressed, very charismatic and confident. He moved fast, spoke and thought quickly—a young sophisticate from the outside.

Taking an honest look at his life was not easy and was something he had avoided. It is easier to make excuses when you don't have to make ones that are specific. He hadn't worked since a stint in the armed services, which is where he said he got introduced to meth. Whether that is true or not, his use was exacerbated there, and he was dishonorably discharged. His mother had been ill for almost two years, however that had not deterred him, and in the interplay between mother and son, they clung to each other, both against their will and at the same time in spite of it.

Without her financial support, he would have had no resources to buy any drugs, so when she tried to withhold money, he stole, begged, borrowed, and cheated. He had no car and still lived at home. She lent him her late-model car, which he drove almost exclusively; she was undergoing aggressive chemotherapy treatments and was too ill to go out. Debt was accumulating, and instead of making wise financial decisions, she made decisions dependant on his happiness and his rights over hers.

How do you tell a mother that she is implicit in her son's continuing choices, when all she does is love him?

Methamphetamine users lie, steal, and cheat as part of who they have become, because they use—they have to because it's a class A drug and attracts prison sentences. It becomes natural to lie; they don't want to get caught. At this point he wasn't who she thought he was, and her wish to see him free wasn't enough.

At our first session it was obvious Jonathon had made his mind up, but in just the first few moments I knew there was not going to be enough reason to stop; it was too easy to keep doing what he had always done. We took stock of his life. As an only child he was big for his age and was always around adults. He was bright and very spoiled, and as he grew up he was told constantly how clever he was and how he could have anything. Jonathon grew up with pressure: how could he live up to the expectations of so many?

Even when he failed consistently through school, college, and then the military, others still saw him as a winner, charismatic and successful, so he became more and more dependent on drugs to manage the superficial front he had become.

Basically Jonathon was self-centered, with no concern for others, caring only for his own pleasure. Jonathon's mother, his greatest support, was dying. This led to more of his devil-may-care attitude. Because he didn't know how to show love to others, because he was so egocentric, he only knew how he felt. What he did about it was to salve his own wounds by numbing his feelings and altering his life with drugs. Because of his looks he was popular, so even his friendships were superficial.

Jonathon had no conscious, painful consequence linked to his drug use. He saw it as a euphoric escape from responsibility and pain. The first answer was for Jonathon to develop a sense of independence, accountability, and accomplishment that had so far evaded him. He had never worked, but he lived well—income, home, phone, and car were provided for him.

He had absolutely no impetus to change, so he was a regular, heavily illicit drug user living in reasonable, easy comfort and financially supported to continue to steal, lie, and cheat to his mother, the person who cared for him most in all his time on earth. She was dying against her will, and he was tempting staying alive by choice. He might have said the words he wanted to change, but I didn't believe that he believed that he had any reason for it to be any different.

He was genuine in saying he wanted to stop, and he *intended* to. I told him to go away, but with a warning, because *wanting is not enough—intention is nothing without action.* Have you ever just intended to do something before, and not done it? After a little reflection, I hoped Jonathon might see and decide that things needed to be different. He did, and we set up a plan of action for him, one that suited him, his situation, and his personality.

A week later, Jonathon started looking for employment. He got up by 8:00 AM, and he made all the necessary phone calls in his job hunt. He avoided his friends, and he was clean and straight. He got a second interview as a sales consultant in a very expensive menswear store, and he soon started work. He met a girl who was drug free and warned him if he used she would leave him. He kept going to his meetings that followed successful rehab. He was king of the hill there, and not being able to help himself, he got back into bragging about how bad he had been, how bad he was, all to a captive audience. He was a big fish in a septic pond

Jonathon broke all the sales records that first fortnight, and as he drove home with his first pay, after his second date, he took a detour and got loaded. He told me he couldn't believe how good he felt, and he bought a bag.

The lazy person who goes to borrow a spade says, "I hope I don't find one."
—SWAHILI SAYING

Chapter Eight
There Is No Silver Bullet

One of the terms I maintain with anybody I work with is once they decide to stop using I will always assume they are drug free. From that moment they become this new identity, and the agreement is they tell me immediately if they take drugs again. Jonathon's mother found his opened bag, and blood all over his shirt from injecting the methamphetamine. She rang me, she was so deeply sad. The last fortnight had given her the most hope she had enjoyed for a long time.

She had relaxed her own behavior again, yearned to trust him, and was expectant. He had not given her any money as he had promised, and he was angry when she confronted him. I waited two days before calling; he ignored me. Until I left a message, knowing he was at work, that I would give him only enough time to get to my office when he finished work to explain what had happened. He rang me, abusive and confrontational (of course), and showed up.

He seemed quite distraught and almost ashamed. Jonathon had been so swept up in his new job and new girl. He had a myriad of excuses for not starting assignments that were required. He was a likeable con. I forgot he was a liar, thief, and cheat.

You do not have to relapse to stop!

After further discussion, he cried. He wanted to start again. He was afraid—afraid of facing his life, afraid of failure, and afraid of being alone. At this point I asked his mother to consider herself over him, sublet her apartment, and stay with friends while she was going through chemo. She wouldn't, so Jonathon took heed; he never missed a day's work, made generous bonuses, and started taking over some of the household expenses. Before I left Australia, Jonathon rang me assuring me while I was away that all would be well.

It had started looking like he was on track, but too soon his excuses started. He didn't bother to complete the assignments or stay away from his old environment and the people even he doesn't refer to as friends. He's still employed, his girlfriend left him, his mother is still dying, he's a druggie, and now without a doubt he knows he is a liar, thief, and cheat, and one day soon it will be too late. I sent this transcript to Jonathon for his comment.

JONATHON'S COMMENTS

There is no silver bullet. I thought I could keep my using under control—what was wrong with a little fun? It hadn't sunk in yet that drugs weren't okay- and methamphetamine was the drug that really messed me up. I got my life back on track quickly, started seeing awesome results at work, met a beautiful woman, and was enjoying life. I felt decent. After a month I got a great commission and bought my mother a flat-screen television, and I know how happy she was to think I had changed my ways.

It would have worked, too, but at that point in a moment of stupidity I got paid and went straight to a dealer. I was feeling so good, I couldn't believe it. I regretted that more than I had before, and thought I could charm my way out of the trouble I had caused again. My girlfriend left me. I had heard those threats from other girls before, so when she did actually do it I was pretty shocked. I lost her; she will not come back, under any circumstances. It seemed that all my luck ran out at once because then I got arrested for vagrancy and drunkenness and put in a cell for twenty-four hours. It was disgusting, and I never want to spend any time in a cell again. I was high but had nothing on me—just a taste of what I didn't want my life to be.

I will start at the beginning again- I know there is no "half way" when it comes to stopping meth—you do or you don't.

Try not. Do, or do not. There is no try.
—YODA, FROM STAR WARS

"Save me" is a slow deliverance; help yourself.
—TSHONA SAYING

Chapter Nine

WIFE, MOTHER, BUSINESS PERSON, JAILBIRD

Helen had been using methamphetamine on and off for almost five years by the time I met her. Before meth, she and her husband, who were both in their forties, owned successful businesses and lived in an expensive home in a good area. Their two older children went to private schools, belonged to tennis and pony clubs, and had music lessons. They apparently enjoyed an affluent, successful life and appeared to be happy. At least that's how it was before methamphetamine, the lying lady.

Helen had started using meth with a single friend, who had been a client who seemed to have a more adventurous life. Helen wanted some of that. She wanted to feel young again and lose a bit of weight. One of the promises meth makes is you will regain your youth and become more desirable, which is hardly the truth as a little bit of time goes by.

Helen took up going to the gym. She went running every day, and Carl was happy that she was spending the time on herself—at first. It's hard to pin down when her behavior went from what could have been a healthy interest to a self-centered obsession, and hindsight as it is, Carl could now recognize things he didn't then that acted as warning signs.

Helen owned a hair and beauty salon. She had enjoyed fifteen years in a prominent address and had four cutters, two therapists, and a business partner, Mark. They had started the business together as friends. Because they had managed a close relationship over the years, Mark had noticed an almost imperceptible change in Helen. He had approached Carl at an earlier stage because things were going wrong, but it was difficult to articulate the changes, and he couldn't put his finger on it exactly at this point. That is why she went so far: nobody knew what to look for and would never have suspected.

It was about three years into using that her business started to suffer. She started to have trouble with staff because she was erratic and unpredictable. The business suddenly had issues with cash-flow problems, and she had crazy, grandiose ideas. She avoided Mark whenever possible because they had started to argue over the day-to-day running of the business. At this point he still trusted her enough to leave the operational side to her, as always; working in a salon, he dismissed the things he was hearing down as gossip.

When she smoked meth, she had the energy to race around all day, stay up late, and, in a burst of thinking, take on new products—bigger and better, she thought, unwittingly sending her loyal traditional suppliers away, owing them money.

Employees that had been with her for years resigned, not knowing what was wrong but knowing something wasn't right.

During this time Helen had plenty of friends she didn't know, most of them younger than her, with nothing in common. Her responsibility toward her family took second place to this new freedom. She told them lies about where she was and didn't bother with the things that had been important—she no longer went to sports or school events, and she increasingly had no time for the things at home that made them a family.

Helen's new friends convinced her to use the salon as a methamphetamine lab: no one would know; they were always using chemicals there anyway. So she did, and a night trade began. Somehow there was little advantage to her, except an increasing supply for herself. The hairdressers would come into the salon and know things had been touched; they were still wondering.

At work—when she turned up—she arrived wired and started to make no sense at all. Like the day she decided people were spying on her, that they were hiding and watching every move she made. So she stayed at the office that night and removed a wall. She fixed them—see, they weren't there now. With no place to hide, they had gone. Good thing she took down the wall.

Her suspicions and paranoia grew along with her use. She ordered more stock but stopped paying for it. They had always enjoyed good credit—not any longer.

The business was a shambles; closing it up was the only solution, and she didn't seem to care. Carl took over the closure, thinking he should have helped more, blaming it on simply too much pressure, still unaware of the truth.

Her old friends were confused; they couldn't quite isolate what was wrong, and when they tried to talk about it, she reacted sharply, so they didn't see her much anymore. She stopped paying the household bills, she had taken the credit cards to their limits, and by now something had to change.

The relationship between her and Carl was at crisis point. Even so, Helen had managed to keep her use a secret, but her increasingly aggressive, erratic behavior that then swung to complete obliviousness had her family bewildered. Carl had no idea that she was using.

Meth convinces its users it is the answer to their life. Helen's use escalated. One moment she seemed to be invincible, the next in the depths of depression, so she looked for the end to her despair in the drug that had caused it. She spent days in bed; her moodiness and detached behavior was put down to hormones. Helen started ignoring everyone else's needs, flying into rages over the simplest things, and hiding the increasingly large withdrawals she was making from their joint account. She had become a liar and cheat.

This drug creeps up on the family and friends unsuspectingly. It's hard to define the cause of the behavior because when something is wrong, we try and find a reason for it. This was different; it was not right, but what?

Her business partner had started the process of ending the relationship and getting out of the business; he contacted Carl. He told him what he knew, and Carl questioned Helen. She didn't deny using, but she was adamant about refusing any help and convinced Carl that she had only touched it once or twice, that she was just in a bad space and she could stop anytime.

She says she kept using because she was exhausted, and she couldn't cope—that's true, because she kept using.

It wasn't the end yet. She continued to use, felt oblivious while on it. When she came down, she raged at the children and was disinterested, cruel, and unthinking toward them.

They were afraid and cried for her, and it got worse.

She became increasingly desperate. Still belligerent, she continued to deny her use. But Carl was watching, still unbelieving but hoping like hell he could find enough of who she used to be to hold onto the hope that nothing had changed.

She then started to inflict pain on herself and started cutting. She kept her arms covered, but Carl inevitably noticed the fresh wounds and thought this was the beginning of her getting the help she needed.

Not quite. She lied and was treated for depression.

She continued using what she could get, and while you couldn't exactly say she was prostituting herself, she had an affair that lasted three months with a guy who became her supplier, and that was the end of her marriage.

Over the next year, Helen's neglect toward her children meant she didn't spend time or occasions with them. Christmas passed without any contact, and birthdays were sometimes late, mostly forgotten, but never as important as what she was doing. And still she lied … and still her family made excuses, hoping against hope that she was not using methamphetamine.

Her elderly mother got Alzheimer's. It was almost a blessing that she hadn't seen the worst of what this drug had stolen from her daughter, son-in-law, and grandchildren. It was a further blessing that Helen was removed from the family trust as a beneficiary and trustee. While going through the court trial, she was furious to know she had no access to her money anymore; she had plans! She felt nothing but rage—no remorse and no consideration toward anyone, just absolute rage when anyone got in her way.

When she was arrested, the police evidence against her included allowing her premises to be used as a clandestine lab, and video footage was provided as evidence. On some nights there were up to thirty short-time visitors, meaning the visit lasted less than five minutes. They had watched her salon for over a year.

The court case and sentencing took over ten months, and after conviction for possession and allowing her premises to be used for manufacture of methamphetamine (and before sentencing), she was held in remand. That's where I met her: in jail, where finally she accepted she could do with help, and she was afraid.

Right up to her time in jail, she had an air of detachment that stopped her facing the truth because she simply forgot how to feel. That's what methamphetamine does, and it hurts her now to look back at what was so easy to destroy, with so little care for anybody but herself; it acts as a reminder. *Her journey back will be difficult but not impossible, but her life will never be the same.* Her children visit her at the medium-security prison she still has two years left in. They see *her* now—no more stories, excuses, or lies. She has done all she can now to make it better and promises to make up for the lost time when she is out.

Will she recover their love? Yes, in part she has, but it is with caution that they will ever trust her again. Can she trust herself is the important question, because that is the answer to any thought of an ongoing relationship with either of them.

Carl and the children have grieved for the loss of their mother; their life is different now. What they assumed was their life and took for granted is no longer. Methamphetamine leaves holes.

Helen was an attractive, successful mother, daughter, wife, and business partner. Now she's a jailbird.

You think it was worth it?

The heart is pounding, and the soul is crashing
FROM A POEM ON THE NET, AUTHOR UNKNOWN

Chapter Ten

THE HEART IS POUNDING; THE SOUL IS CRASHING

BRUCE AND SUE

A friend rang me, asking for help for a friend who had a bit of a problem with taking pain killers. When Bruce turned up at my office and stood at the doorway, he was yellow. He had taxed his liver to the point where he was not well now but was going to be very sick, very soon. Bruce was smoking methamphetamine four or five times every day, and had been for three years. He took forty Nurofen daily to act as an opiate and to calm him. He was spending more than two thousand dollars some weeks on methamphetamine, and hundreds a week on pain killers.

Bruce was a successful broker and had earned a top position in a large investment company. He was articulate and extremely intelligent (not withstanding his current idiocy of course). He met his wife of seven years at a party. Both were smashed at the time, and their marriage was of young professional, recreational drug users.

Two children came along, and Sue left her career at a television production house. Her resentment increased as her responsibility as a wife and mother grew. I got the impression she was a little jealous of him, certainly of the continued success he enjoyed and freedom he took while she stayed at home.

Now, four years since they met, Bruce's behavior at work was starting to show him up through mistakes, bursts of anger, irrational decisions, and frequent absences while he binged. His use escalated—he dealt with other people's money. His failing job performance had serious implications, and the company he worked for had suspicions but no proof of his use. Then his wife threatened to leave him and exposed a little of the story to his boss's wife. Bruce came to me because a friend sent him. Sue had herself always taken drugs. In her opinion, it was Bruce's use that had gotten out of control. His libido was low, and there was no level of intimacy on any basis any longer. Their mutual drug days were over, and so was their marriage from her point of view.

Sue was watching the matrimonial possessions and investments vanish and wanted her share from their loveless marriage that had been built on drugs.

Bruce and Sue came to the office ostensibly to try and reconcile their differences. He was living on the couch at a friend's house and was increasingly uncomfortable. He was still using and lying about it.

His personality was a difficult one. He was highly articulate, he was perceptive and expressive, and on meth he was invincible, untouchable, arrogant, and very sick. His body was about to shut down. His wife had changed the rules— no longer was his using acceptable—and he was hanging on a thread at work. I had to undergo an interview process with her and her mother. Sue took a sanctimonious stance. I guess that was her schoolteacher training.

Between her and her mother there was a necessary silence, a facade that they kept up all the way. Families keep secrets, and this was one. Their marriage breakdown was his fault, not hers.

Sue made it a condition of coming that we did not address her use. I suspected she was waiting for a property that was owned by him to sell and a term investment to mature before she left him, and saying she had gone with him to drug counseling sounded like just what the judge wanted to hear. Her settlement would be more favorable. I know they were no longer good for each other, and they had children.

Two hurt, angry, and self-centered people came to my office: him feeling guilty enough to shoulder all the blame of a marriage they had destroyed together, and her vindictive enough to do so. In those early days, it always erupted into a screaming rage; the children had to be taken out of the office. If what they did publicly acted as any indication, then they were better off apart. While Sue sought support from her family, Bruce was estranged from his.

Bruce was lucky to have had friends who provided him with a place to stay. He took a month's leave, and we started his journey back to sanity. He was very sick, and we arranged a three-hour appointment with a homeopath, who provided us a list of trace elements and herbs to ease his nausea and stop his sugar demands, and then we enforced a retreat on Bruce. We sent him away with no access to a phone, transport, or drugs. He had to cook for himself, had no television, and couldn't concentrate enough to read.

In the evening a registered nurse would spend time with him, to see that he was safe, but not take over his duties. He had to hit the ground and start again from the most basic level. He missed his children, wanted to reconcile, and decided to get fit again. At this point, at least, his health was returning, and in three days he went back to his friend's place.

I asked Bruce to do three things that would keep his recovery on track: *First, that he stay at his friend's* and fit in to the family life; that meant getting up in the morning and sleeping at night, eating well, and helping out around the house. Secondly, *that he exercise every day,* without fail; he was gaining weight rapidly, as his body was detoxing. Thirdly, *that he stay away from his friends who took or dealt drugs.* Bruce agreed, and between his friend and a few people chosen for their experience and training, we watched him work the drugs out of his system. I wish this could have had a much easier ending, but this was only the beginning, and it would take a while longer before Bruce's life was completely on track.

Sue and Bruce were each implicit in the other's behavior, and when she demanded he come back it was so he could take over the childcare and household responsibility that she had had enough of. It was also expected he would continue his high level of income. Bruce's body was breaking down, and the more stress he faced, the more he sought to escape.

Methamphetamine is not an escape; it is a trap.

Against good advice and because he missed his boys, who were very young, he moved back into his family home, and their violent arguing continued. Neither of them seemed capable of breaking the pattern of behavior they were in. I became a handy scapegoat. Sue argued and defied everything I asked of them; she transferred a lot of the blame from Bruce toward me. I wonder when she knew she was losing him.

This is where the dynamic interplay between people is often astounding. As Bruce started to gather himself, started to see clearly and straight, Sue had to either keep lying to herself, or start to address her own responsibility. She pushed for the first.

Because of her own guilt, she attacked me. Bruce was still pretty paranoid and angry, so it was easy to convince him I was the source of his problems. While he continued to see me, he was obstructive and offensive. I would have to start all over again every time I saw him, making his steps small and less rewarding.

Sue spent a lot of money, went out with friends, played tennis, and ate lunch out all the time. Almost unbelievably, she had friends over for dinner and at our next session Bruce mentioned they took ecstasy that night—he says he didn't. At this point Bruce was hoping he could make it all better, and when Sue asked him to stop seeing me, it worked. Not completely, because he kept coming quite irregularly, and he just didn't tell her. But neither did he do any of the things necessary at the time.

Later we found these friends had testified against him and used this evening as proof he never stopped using. As a consequence and as expected, she appeared a wounded victim, and the courts treated her favorably when they decided the custody of the children and the financial settlements a little later on.

Bruce started back at work but stopped exercising, saying he was too busy, too stressed, had no time anymore. And as he had previously, he used this as his excuse to start using again and then lie about it. It took a few weeks before we could be sure. Brucewas asked to attend a workshop over the next three months, every second weekend.

Nobody else attending knew of Bruces use; what was relevant were the self-help tools and strategies that were being offered.

He came to the workshop smashed, and in the company of other participants he twisted the content that was being delivered and vied for power with the presenter, and was rude and arrogant and argumentative. At the end of the first weekend, it was clear he was using methamphetamine, and to his self-righteous dismay he was censured and told not to come back—remember, users like to think that nobody notices, that nothing has changed.

I sent Bruce an email detailing my feelings and reiterating my decision. He left it in the printer tray at work and to his relief (because he was up against a wall), his employer saw it, and he was let go, with a generous final payout. But Bruce was still on a path of self-destruction...

Bruce became aggressive and wouldn't respond to my calls. He accused the people who had taken responsibility for his care of taking drugs while he was detoxing. He was irresponsible and took advantage of anyone he could. He bad mouthed and discredited everybody who had helped him.

Six weeks after starting his recovery, Sue caught him in the garage smoking meth. He moved back to his friend's place. Sue and Bruce fought over their assets for the next three months, and between them the lawyers won. Their marriage had nothing left to save. He hadn't disclosed how much money he had been paid out honestly, but close to thirty thousand dollars was gone on meth in just over two months.

Bruce was an accomplished liar, and he had the ability to use words as weapons and tools. To himself, he put up a rational argument for continuing to completely destroy his life and family.

Again I challenged the complicity I see. Bruce's employer knew of his use, and it was irresponsible of him to pay him such a big cash bonus. Bruce was in no position to bargain. If his employer, who knew everything by this time, had said it was to go into a trust until he was well, that may have made a big difference to his imminent recovery.

Instead Bruce had a lot of cash and thought he had nothing left to fight for. His arrogance only masking the feeling he held for himself. I suppose he thought he wasn't worth the fight, yet ...

While it didn't happen magically and it wasn't the easy road, Bruce was on a path toward freedom, starting to see the reality of his world. A significant experience was at about this time he went to his dealer to find the man had been beaten to a pulp: the dealer's arm was broken, a guitar was smashed over his head, and his house was trashed—all over a late payment. Suddenly the world of recreational drugs and parties had lost its glamour.

Sue moved to be closer to her family and got custody of the children. He followed her up the country and got a new job, with no damage to his reputation. They stayed apart, but it still took a friend to come over every morning and get him up and get him ready for work, then drive him (still pretty belligerent every morning for weeks) to work, to see that he had food, and to check in on him at night.

Slowly he started working on the pieces of his life that mattered most. The courts decided the role he would play in his children's lives. He attended to his health and his diet, and he started to plan a little. As an ironic twist he had found himself in an apartment above a meth lab, so he moved.

Did he start doing the exercises he was asked to do? He made no attempt, not consciously anyway, and in fact he was happy to blame the fact on not receiving the information sooner. Remember that some months previously he had been given the opportunity to work through all the tools. He was also invited to pick it back up at anytime.

A year later Bruce is not touching drugs, he does not smoke methamphetamine, he is fit, and he is doing well in his career. It wasn't easy for him, but it could have been easier. When asking him about their relationship, a year after their split, his wife had asked him to reconcile, and because he has refused, and with much disgust, she holds the view that he hasn't learned a thing.

Bruce was lucky to have started the way he did, to have had the support he had, and once shown again how life could be, in his own way he achieved freedom. He has nothing left; his wife got most of the marriage settlement, so he is working hard to make up and buy a place to live again. He has a close relationship with his parents again now. Though he is still scathing at times, he is much happier but worried for his children. His boys? As described by

Bruce, one is a chronic liar, and the other shifts between being both a bully and a victim. You see, our actions are never without consequence …

Bruce and Sue, you know who you are. I hope seeing your story written this way gives you both one more sharp kick. It's not too late to start protecting your kids from what they have seen as an example—and it's not too early, either.

Chapter Eleven

TONY

As so frequently happens, I was approached by Tony's mother. She was of course in distress; she had watched her son's life start to really fall apart. At twenty-six, he had three children and was living with one of their mothers part-time. He was on a court-imposed curfew, awaiting trial on charges of assault, dangerous use of a vehicle, and shoplifting, which he had turned into a trade to buy drugs; dope, and methamphetamine.

His mother had recently lost her husband (Tony's stepfather), and she desperately wanted her son back. She simply didn't know who he was anymore.

Tony had started taking drugs at fourteen, dropped out of school, and started drifting. His mother describes him as having been a typical, bright, and happy kid, but he became rude and unhappy at that point. He began to steal from her and his stepfather and started shoplifting.

One night his young girlfriend of the time came in and confided to Julia that she was afraid of him and worried. He had severe mood swings, alternately aggressive and depressed, always looking for something. On the evening in question he was wasted on alcohol, dope, and speed, then while in the city, he stripped naked and ran onto a busy street, throwing himself at cars.

When he was restrained, he was angry and fought the people subduing him, crying that he meant to be good, he just didn't know how. He was psychiatrically assessed at that point and diagnosed differently, from being manic, depressed, and schizophrenic. He was treated for attention deficit disorder.

In actuality he was already taking every illegal drug available, so the cocktail of prescription drugs he was put on just fed his craziness. He was out of control, and as belligerence had become the only style he used to communicate with his parents, they decided to send him to his birth father.

He stopped his prescribed medication. His use of drugs, however, was constant, and his use of amphetamine-based drugs increased. Here he was now, twelve years later, on house curfew and awaiting trial for burglary and for failing to stop for the police.

He had manufactured methamphetamine until his arrest; knowing he was under surveillance and unable to leave his house, he stopped. He still got methamphetamine as often as possible, but now that he couldn't shoplift as easily anymore, he had no way to pay for his drug, and his desire was about to cost him more than he had bargained for.

When you owe money to the gangs that control the distribution of meth, and you think you are okay with them, they will surprise you. They will get the money you owe them. With baseball bats, they will give you a good beating as a first warning, then they will threaten your family.

This is one of the situations that lead users to taking their lives: the situation becomes too much and too big, and there's no apparent way out. That's why you feel so bad: you have no strategy for it to be better, the drug you think you need has dried up, and you owe money to dangerous people who won't think twice about what they will do to get it back. Any surprises? Not nice? You're right; you are playing with a class A illicit drug. You can go to jail because of it, and so can they. So if it means them or you, they are prepared to do to you and your loved ones what they've done many times before, to others. Why act as if you can't believe it could happen to you?

There is a simple, big-picture solution: stop the demand! It gets even simpler, so stop your demand for it.

Tony's manner was quite pleasant at first. I arrived with his mother to a house he shared with his father and most recent girlfriend and baby, who stayed over more often than not.

The house was in filthy condition. Two dogs were on chains at the front entrance, their feces littering the walk up to the door. Inside it stunk of stale cigarette smoke. There were stacks of papers and empty soda bottles everywhere. The floor was covered in animal hair. The baby slept in a room with clothing piled high on the bed, no fresh air, curtains pulled, and the TV going. Tony was sloppy, and his clothes were dirty. He had a laissez-faire attitude, seemed to be quite confident, and at the same time he was increasingly uncomfortable and offended with me turning up.

Tony and his mother were a perfect pair. He played on her guilt and blamed her for his bad behavior because she left his father, moved to another state, and married someone else who he didn't like, then sent him back to his father. Anything he could lay on her he did, and she took it. Basically, at his worse Tony was behaving as if he was lazy, spoilt, and selfish, and didn't give a damn.

That makes sense, he started screwing himself over so young that he had few choices. He didn't know what or how to do much of anything. He was unemployed because he had no job. He was lazy because he sat around all day. He acted like he didn't give a damn because he was afraid.

When I coach people, I observe their behavior. If they are extreme, I look at what the opposite behavior is, knowing they are capable of an equal swing that way.

When you are fighting to restore your soul's equilibrium after choosing such an evil drug, it is natural to fall into a state of remorse; that's balance, that's physics, that's nature working. It is a reality check.

The other way I understand my clients is to exaggerate their behavior. People are capable of good, and they are capable of bad. We are each capable of both.

He had stolen money and jewelry from his mother and had used up a considerable inheritance, and his mother was prepared to wear what should have been his shame for a life he had wasted so much of, so far.

Successful recovery most often involves more than one person, Tony and his mother had been doing a dance for his whole life. He was an adored only child, and she wanted him to have everything she could provide. She was a lovely person, truly gentle and kind and caring. He saw her as weak, a sucker, and an easy touch, and deep down he was as angry with himself as with her. Every time she gave into him, he liked them both less.

It was not an incredible compulsion to use methamphetamine we had to tackle, but his behavior as a person that needed to be adjusted and challenged, with new behaviors put in place—along with hers.

How do I know that? Because when he can get cocaine, LSD, ketamine, or ecstasy, he uses that; he prefers them in that order, but it's too expensive. Now that he can't get out as much to steal, marijuana is frequently available. If he can't afford methamphetamine, which is his current fifth preference, he smokes dope. He also says proudly he doesn't touch heroin. That's kind of like making choices, don't you think?

Tony is an escape artist, but now the inevitable remorse is kicking in. He does have responsibility now: he has children, and his mother's change of attitude toward him is starting to be evident. His old behavior wasn't working anymore; he had no money and realized he had no genuine friends left, and he would most likely go to jail and spend more time in home detention. Starting to feel a little pain maybe?

Our first meeting, which lasted three hours, went well. I met his girlfriend and saw how involved he was in his son's upbringing. He seemed remorseful and guilt ridden—neither of which was a particularly helpful emotions.

Basically, Tony had paid a price for using drugs so early in his developmental stages—he was still like a kid. When I commented on the state of his house, he started rushing around, tidying and straightening things like a kid sent to clean his room. He had arrested his development at about fourteen years—he still lived with his father, watched TV all day, and played with his boy as if he was a doll. Tony had only worked sporadically; he had spent time on the job with his dad as a builder some five years ago, but he stole his father's tools and sold them to buy drugs, so he was no longer welcome, and his father needed convincing.

He labored over his circle of life, and in his words, it all looked quite sad. As a man, provider, father, and son, he wasn't rating too highly—he hadn't looked at it like that before.

At this first session, after his initial annoyance, Tony was starting to see the reason for me being there. We discussed all of his dreams and aspirations in relation to how he was living currently and how it would need to be. Over the afternoon, he apologized to his mother and committed to doing whatever it would take to stop using. I didn't believe him entirely—being a little dramatic and crying was part of how he had got away with all he had. He had a little charisma and was adept at manipulation, especially regarding his mother and father.

As soon as I left he rang his mother and abused her and ridiculed me, saying I had nothing to offer him. He could stop anytime he wanted to, and I had to leave him alone. I knew success was close.

Transformation can happen over days, weeks, months—or in an instant. It is entirely how you want it to be.

Tony did stop manufacturing and using meth immediately. He was lazy in his nature and character from the years of smoking marijuana, and methamphetamine had taken him to a delusional world where he was ten feet tall and invincible. He hadn't enjoyed much success of his own making, and smoking meth created such a lie in his life that reality didn't come into it before now.

After the façade lifted, Tony actually started to enjoy talking and planning in each area. By the end of our session he was quite clear, and at least he had a better idea of how it could be different. One of the decisions he made was to go to work with his father, if he would have him.

Tony was feeling it was all under his control when I left. I had met his girlfriend Sian, who was there at the time, and of the two, it appeared she had a much stronger character. She was more driven, was sharper, had higher expectations, was more educated, and had wealthy parents. Still only nineteen years old, she spent most of her time with the baby at Tony's house, claiming government assistance while also enjoying the benefits of living at home with her parents.

Her parents had her going to a drug and alcohol rehab program. She dutifully attended but used methamphetamine with Tony every opportunity she could. Her face and body was covered in sores, and she was nervy yet sullen. She assured me she only did it because he did, and she could stop anytime. It was pretty obvious that they both had to stop using, and what she was doing wasn't working either.

At first it appeared Tony wanted to clean it up, but Sian had no such intention—not immediately anyway. She was a very powerful influence in his life. She was very agreeable while I was there, but I knew as part of the dance they were in, he didn't have the guts to stand up against her. What Tony didn't know is when and as soon as she could meet someone else, she would take their child, and because of his record, she would get awarded custody, and he wouldn't see his children, and that's the way it would go.

Tony was lacking in character; he started to use drugs at a stage of his life when he was defining his identity, so drugs were defining him. He would have to build his character, so after he agreed to work with me further, we shook hands and made a promise that he would do whatever it takes to stop the drugs.

Methamphetamine does not care about you, or who you are, or what you become while you use it.

Every area of Tony's life had been influenced by his extensive drug use. He was isolated and antisocial because of it. He had never learned the skills necessary for friendships, and he hadn't learned fairness, respect, and trust. He had never even played sports at school, which he didn't finish. He was lacking mental muscle and didn't know how to expect more. He had never fit into any conventional way of living. He had three children from three different mothers, all supported by the government with no shame. He didn't work, and he spent his day lying around smashed as often as he could. At this point the impetus to change was too insignificant—he had a home, his father provided food and money, and while his supply was dwindling he was still getting methamphetamine.

Until his mother arranged a visit against his will and as a complete ambush. But that day, in spite of themselves, both he and Sian saw enough reason to change and enough trust to know they could do it. It really doesn't take much.

Chapter Twelve

WANTING MORE

Sian was at Tony's first session, which out of necessity was at his place because of his house arrest. It was two days later that Sian's parents got a phone call at 6:00 AM to come and get her and the baby. Previously when Sian, upset over a fight with Tony, had rung her parents and asked that they get her, she would quickly retract her request. Not this time; Sian had started a change, and she wanted out. Her sessions would now be from her family home, separate from Tony with the intention they would stay apart until they could be together.

After the initial agreement to see me, Sian went off the idea. However I arranged with her parents to just turn up at their house when she didn't expect me. The best idea was to see Tony and Sian apart to determine whether they could be together during the process. For things to be different, they each had to make the same decision, and if they were going to be together for their child's sake, they needed to work together toward the same goals.

She asked me not to mention her use to either of their parents. I never make promises that protect users! Recovery works when you tell the truth, *and if there are consequences, too bad.*

One of the ironies here is the fact that the user asks you to remain complicit with them and keep their secret from people that know anyway, and they seem genuinely surprised when their "trust" is breached.

The other widespread behavior I see frequently is that when talking to groups, they mention among themselves how someone they know needs help, but they won't give a name or broach the subject because that person would be devastated if he or she knew they knew.

Sian's parents were well aware that their talented, bright, and beautiful daughter was throwing her life away. They knew she took drugs but not the extent to which she used; they just knew it was a terrible problem that wasn't going to just go away. As much as they held hope that this would be the time that made the difference, they were skeptical and disbelieving because nothing had worked in the past.

They blamed Tony, but the truth was Sian had started doing drugs at fourteen; she left school because of it. Her parents were unable to cope with her, so they excused her, as long as she kept up a reasonable façade and they could blame someone else for their daughter's behavior.

Tony and Sian were together with only two things in common at this point: a baby and methamphetamine use. It had not started that way; while they had both used drugs when they met, methamphetamine was something they started using together.

When they say they loved their baby, they didn't mean it enough to provide her a safe home, one without residue of the toxic smoke. They didn't mean it enough to stop their erratic parenting and the increasingly violent arguments that had become more frequent and threatening. When Tony failed to even attempt any of the actions I asked of him, Sian started to see where they were going, and suddenly she wanted a life with more promise for her and her baby.

She had her parents to escape to, but she would not get off lightly—her family had decided how things were going to be, and there were new expectations. She was used to coming home to them wasted and needing to sleep for days, paying little attention to Chloe, still only five months old.

Up until now, Sian had been able to leave her baby with her parents whenever she wanted. Her parents supported the baby, buying all her clothes and toys and paying for any medical expenses necessary. That left Sian with her government assistance to buy drugs, a little dope, and methamphetamine. At times she would be so aggressive that it frightened her parents; now they were starting to worry about the threat of violence toward Chloe.

The use of methamphetamine is implicated in the most horrific murders, especially children, who are helpless and willing victims. People become violent and irrational when they use meth, and paranoid and psychotic if they don't stop. Remember a factor here is there is no quality check; you get what you get, and you never know what it will be.

So after the first session with Tony, Sian had woken up to having more, and his world was starting to fall down around him. His past strategy had been to threaten suicide at times like this, to call his mother to cry and yell at her that he would take his life. He hadn't so far. As far as I could see, he was taking a fair bit of hers every time, and each time she had reacted, he had got his way, with her giving him money usually as a response to one of his demands. This is a serious situation, but what is the money for?

This is one of those calls you must make sometimes as the partner/family of the user. Remember, they are not behaving in a rational, logical way. They are adept at lying and manipulating; this is their way. You love them and want them to be better. You have a couple of choices here: succumb to their threats, which usually are requests for money, as they worsen, turn outward, and then get their violence directed at you as things worsen for them; or call their bluff.

Methamphetamine makes people who you were close to do things they wouldn't normally. Users are not aware and don't care for things they used to, and when the money runs out and the supplier is putting on the pressure, they will turn on you and make threats against you. They do not care anymore for anyone but themselves. They are not acting like the person they used to be, so stop treating them like that. Face the reality; the facts are in front of you. Protect yourself from what is happening to you because of them, because they will not.

If you do not address the user's underlying beliefs, patterns, and behaviors, they will not understand enough to change their lives effectively. When recovery is not complete, users crave, their behavior degrades again, and they go back to using because they can't find enough reason not to. When users go back to the drug, it is because they have done a deal with themselves: they will do it differently this time. Often other people become involved who offer bad advice and encourage the user.

In the Philippines, the crab catchers use buckets to collect crabs. They don't have lids on them, and it is pretty obvious the crabs could quite easily climb out. The reason why they don't use lids is they collect two crabs at first, put them in the bucket, and know after that a lid is superfluous, because once there are more than two crabs in the bucket, the crabs at the bottom will prevent any other crab's escape by pulling them back down.

Stopping meth use does not mean you will stop doing things that are wrong, but you have no reason to blame it on methamphetamine anymore.

Chapter Thirteen

SIAN

Sian was only nineteen, had been smoking methamphetamine for almost six years, had a baby and a king-size attitude, and was used to getting her own way. She was obviously bright, although she hadn't done well at school, and now as a mother she was lazy and neglectful—and she had no intention of giving up.

She was furious when she discovered her parents had arranged for me to turn up and work with her. She came from an affluent family who had all been close and had no answers to why she had done the things she had when she had been given all the opportunity to have and achieve anything she wanted.

The morning she left Tony was due to a fight about changing the baby, each screaming at the other they were lazy. The fact is they had both been stirred, thinking about the way things were, and how they could be different. Tony seemed the more complacent of the two at first, but after an introspective glance he had made his mind up: he was not going to use methamphetamine any longer.

He started immediately to clean the house, throwing out rotting rubbish bags that had sat for months at the front step. He cleaned out the refrigerator and dumped dozens of empty soda bottles. He rearranged the furniture, vacuumed, and removed the animal mess. His intentions and his actions were congruent—he had started a transformation, instantly repairing his damaged mind by seeking his own reward through a little bit of hard work.

Then, two days later, he and Sian had a fight over responsibilities. Ironic it's true, but that's where it was at: right at the beginning and very basic.

After ringing her parents and saying she wanted them to pick her up, she rang again telling them it was all right. I asked that they go and get her anyway and bring her home.

On leaving Tony's house, and after a fight over taking the baby, Sian had her first scheduled session with me. I had also spent three hours with Tony earlier that day. They both accused the other of being the worst offender and instigator. It was all the other person's fault, and of course they insisted that meth was just for fun and they could stop anytime.

It had now been five days since they had last used. Each was on their own path, with their own motivation to stop: Sian because she could see opportunities ahead for her, and Tony because he was tired of things the way they were.

Tony's curfew allowed him to go to work with his father, who, after seven years of Tony's unemployment, agreed to give him a second chance. Tony got a job as a laborer on a construction site.

A week later I spent time with him, his third session. The house was tidy, and he had plans for building a tent for the kids to sleep outside the next weekend. His skin looked better, and he could look directly at me when I spoke. This didn't mean it was without fallout; his father was a drinker and verbally abusive at best—this seems a little crazy, but it's not so complex.

Tony would now look at his father with little respect, reflect his own behavior, and reinforce his own change. His father hadn't managed to curb his excessive drinking and drunken, aggressive behavior, ever.

Tony was not in the best environment, but it worked for him, reminding him of his own wasted years and how good he felt with the idea of getting it all together, so despite of and because of his surroundings, Tony stayed committed to not touching methamphetamine again.

While Tony loved his father and appreciated him for providing a roof over his head, he didn't want to be like his father anymore.

He had made a decision to make it better, and he felt better, so in his relationship with his mother he started to tell the truth again. She said for as long as she could remember, and for the first time in years, he was treating and speaking to her with respect. I guess that was his returning.

Sian

Sian stayed at her parents. She had realized they were better apart for the moment, and he was working now, so his days were full. When he worked on a building site around the corner from her family home, she took him lunch, something that required more thoughtfulness than either of them had displayed a few weeks ago.

Over this time there were a couple of incidences, one where Tony's father stormed through the house, angry and drunk, shouting abuse at Tony. A few weeks later, and against the bond conditions placed on him, Tony and his father went out. Tony left the house where his father was drinking and went on a shoplifting spree with two cousins. This time they got caught. They went to court the next day, and astonishingly he got away with a fine.

This they kept secret from me. I think he got away with a false name and address, and that shows you how stressed the judicial system is; the conditions of his bond meant he should have been jailed instantly until trial. I suspect Tony will take a while longer before he turns his life around in all areas. He will always be torn between trying to be his father's son and seeking approval from him.

His father's abuse toward him has continued. It's always the same: when he's drunk, he unleashes all the rage he has inside for himself toward Tony. While this has made it harder, it has served a good lesson, and Tony has had to experience and manage an unreasonable, out-of–control, and erratic relationship. It is a lesson in irony, along with patience and self-discipline. It was five weeks since our first meeting, and David and Sian were both free of methamphetamine.

Sian's parents' expectations of her changed too; she had to become more accountable for her baby's cares. She was less argumentative and aggressive as every day went by. Her mother said she was happy and more considerate, and acting more like the daughter they knew.

I think it is human nature to get away with what we can, and in today's world, where immediate self-gratification is king, there is little accountability for others anymore. We become reckless. Sian had taken a look behind her and no longer liked what she saw.

That didn't mean her parents trusted her absolutely, weren't afraid, or could forget what she put them through. It was difficult for them to trust her even a little bit, and they held their breath, instinctively waiting for the next blow, for a while. At a point they thought she was safe, they faced their own feelings of hurt, anger, and resentment at what she done to them, her sisters, their husbands, her grandparents, her cousins, and her friends she had disappointed, offended, and hurt.

Both families had to negotiate the changes, accepting that for the first time in a long time they not only could but had to trust Sian's and Tony's decisions. Sian, while still living with her mother and father, had the freedom to see Tonyand take the baby on the weekends, now that Tonywas working.

Sian had to accept more responsibility for Chloe's care, and her mother had to let go of the control she still felt entitled to. You can't trust, believe, or forgive a little bit—you either do or you don't.

We continued to work through the tools, and neither of them has ever used methamphetamine again. Shortly after we started working together, Sian helped me in the office and now has almost finished a degree that she started two years ago.

Tony doesn't steal anymore, something he had done as a living for ten years. He has plans to save some money and go back to where he went to school, find a small cottage to live in, and have his children stay, because he has a room for them. Maybe he and Sian will work out, maybe they won't, but life is better right now for everyone. They didn't have to do much for it to be this way; they just find a reason to stop that was good enough and do it!

Neither Tony nor Sian found their nirvana in all those years of taking drugs. Methamphetamine had the most devastating effect on them both, and it is ironic it became his savior, in a funny kind of way: after years of drugs, it was methamphetamine that drove him to getting the help he needed.

Maybe that is what this epidemic is all about, because methamphetamine use causes unacceptable things to happen. Maybe we will take a stand against it and stop the supply and demand. How long will it take?

Sian and Tony were preparing to live together when I finished seeing them. They had to save for tenancy and utility bonds and a car. Then Tony can apply for a license to drive to work and back again until his sentence is served. They are making up for lost time, and finally, at twenty-six, David will leave home for the first time, be financially independent, and able to support Sian and their baby.

Chapter Fourteen
THERE ARE ALWAYS VICTIMS

The next stories focus on some of the trials and tribulations the families of methamphetamine users face. While the user apparently doesn't care, can't care, or won't care, there are responsibilities that arise, and they often fall on the family to deal with.

Frequently the user has kept away, so while the family knew something was wrong, they had no idea of the extent of the situation. Sometimes the user has kept up a façade, and the family only finds out if there are criminal charges.

There are always innocent victims, always.

KEN AND MARGARET'S STORY

Ken and Margaret were both in their late sixties when they discovered they were on the verge of bankruptcy—their son had taken over as managing director when they retired from their thriving trucking company. He had managed to hide huge cash transfers, but the annual reports for the last two years called for an internal audit, and he couldn't hide it any longer.

His parents had to sell property to float the business. He was a shareholder and a recipient of the trust, and by law they had to pay him out one third of everything they sold to recoup his theft. They were proud of the reputation they had earned over thirty-eight years of doing business, and this was almost too much to suffer. They tried to contest his legal right to inherit the money, but they had nothing to stand on, even though they told the police of their son's use.

While they were trying to stall him and avoid paying out, he moved into a gang headquarters. He wouldn't return phone calls to anyone in his family, and he became even more abusive and threatening. He sent text messages threatening to kill them and then himself and burn down their home and the business.

His mother rang me when she was desperate and aching for the son she used to know. The extent of their estrangement means it has been impossible to meet him to talk—all she could do is get on with other things and forget him, hoping that one day he will listen to reason again and get the help he needs. How does this happen to a family that has provided everything?

He kept up the assault while they tried to hold off the transfer of the money. They had no grounds, so they resigned themselves to paying him off, even though they knew the grip the gang had over him. They agreed, but before the legal work was done, he rang his mother begging for an advance of twenty thousand dollars. He was desperate to get the money, and out of his need he did what was necessary: he was nice to his mother, and she set herself up once more to suffer another blow.

He asked about the family for the first time in over twenty months. He said he would visit them on the weekend. He said everything a mother who can't believe what has happened to her son can believe, because she wanted to.

He told her if he didn't have the money he owed by the next day he would be in danger and would be seriously hurt by gang members. He went from the callous, aggressive, and vile-mouthed person to the son she knew. He cried a little, acted afraid, and for all of twenty minutes, while they stood in a car park and hugged for the first time in more than two years, she believed what he was saying.

So against my advice she met him at her solicitors' office and advanced a payment to him. He took the money, the payout followed, and that was the last she saw of him until his arrest.

I believe we had a small opportunity there to talk him into getting help. We could have met him in the car park as arranged. Knowing he had no money, he would be coming down, less excitable, and maybe a little ashamed. They knew I was against relenting on the money and in favor of forcing him to have to take them to court for his payout, but his mother wanted everything to be magically okay.

It's a hard lesson, isn't it?

At the point of writing this, three months have gone by, and almost half a million dollars in money that has been paid out to him has gone. He has vanished from them, and they have heard nothing since. There is no doubt the money went into manufacturing methamphetamine. He is still driving his expensive company car and using his phone, they know that because they get the bills .His mother hasn't the heart to disconnect the phone because it is the last remnant of contact but he doesn't answer her calls. His cousin told them he has shaved his head to look more like the other members of the gang he is affiliated to. His face is covered in sores, and he is looking pretty scrawny and damaged.

It has served as a cruel lesson, and Margaret has directed her focus on her other son and his children. It is all she can do until he makes contact again. When that happens, she will expect more from him.

I hope he doesn't leave it too late.

Some weeks after writing this, the police performed a major raid on the gang headquarters, and he was among the sixty-three people arrested for manufacturing and supplying methamphetamine, money laundering, and dealing in stolen property. Help for him seems too late, for now anyway.

If you have hoped and your expectation was not fulfilled, then go on hoping.
THE TALMUD

ANDREA'S STORY

Five years ago, Andrea's brother didn't turn up at Christmas lunch.

In fact the family hadn't seen much of him at all over the previous year. He had changed, though he had always been a little selfish. In his forties with no kids of his own, he had not had a lot of responsibility toward anyone else. He had never been too involved as an uncle, brother, or son.

He owned a successful advertising agency and was known for his creative, fast-thinking style.

When he first started to ignore family invitations, the family thought he was just distracted; they had heard rumors that his business wasn't going so well. He was pretty independent, so there weren't really a lot of warning signs as to what was going to happen.

It is easier to see in retrospect how he could have been helped if Andrea had faced her fears at the time. She had concerns, but time went by and the distance between them grew.

Then her father got ill, and the lawyer contacted her about the family trust, which needed attention. Her brother was a trustee and had written his own business losses off against the trust. He had also withdrawn a very large amount of money without any explanation to anybody and without any consent; he just forged their signatures.

When Andrea found out, she approached him. He denied it, and when she showed him evidence, he refused to talk about it any more. That's when things got crazy. She contacted his business partner. He told her Simon had "lost it" and had run the business into the ground; the business partner was out. In his own words, when Simon started bringing his shit and the crack whores he was hanging around with into work, that was all the warning he needed. He was out after fifteen years of a successful business together because Simon was smoking methamphetamine and couldn't or wouldn't stop.

The "crack whores" were a string of young girls that moved into his very expensive home, and over time there were two paternity claims to explain their pregnancies and births while they lived with him. He supported both girls and their babies, buying them clothing, furniture, food, money, and methamphetamine in exchange for a stab at being half his age again.

The first time around, he introduced the young girl to Andrea, who kept her comments to herself about the obvious age and intellectual gap in the relationship. She was happy to think maybe he would settle down again. Simon was a father and she was an aunty. Maybe everything would be all right, and this would set him straight.

Her teenagers thought they had a new cousin and visited when they could, bringing presents and telling their friends.

Simon had a paternity test when the mother's boyfriend turned up and expected to move in to the house.

Neither baby proved to be his, to his disappointment. The rift got deeper between him and Andrea. He got into more financial trouble and all the while his ideas got bigger, and his demands for money got louder.

He lost interest in having anything to do with the family. Andrea's kids had lost any respect toward him, but Andrea still denied the extent of the damage done and turned a blind eye to the future. He tried to avoid her; frequently he would pretend not to be home when she called around to discuss his affairs that had to be put right. A degree of shock had set in.

She still would not believe he was using methamphetamine, instead believing he was just a victim to some lying, unfair cops who had it in for him. Her elderly father's health deteriorated, and there was more pressure on her to manage the situation they were in. She was alone and couldn't speak to anyone about it because she felt ashamed and guilty for the things he had done.

Simon had invested her parents' trust money in race horses, involving himself in some high flyers, and it got worse.

He hadn't filed their tax returns as had been his responsibility, and they were being audited, causing enormous stress to his father, an upright citizen for all his life.

Simon continued to deny any use, and Andrea bought into his stories, even when he told her he was having problems with painted moths invading his body and coming out his ears. She knew that was pretty crazy, but in the midst of everything else it was just another thing to excuse; she simply did not want to see the truth because it was too hard to believe.

Three years after he missed Christmas lunch, police raided his house, and he got arrested for possession and supply.

While he was waiting for sentencing, he was put under house arrest. He was angry, still blaming the police for his business failure. He convinced his sister the police were corrupt, that he was innocent and wasn't doing it anymore. So over the next year, to avoid his house being foreclosed, she mortgaged hers, and he continued to use. He owed money for his supply, his house got robbed and trashed, and he got beaten and then tried to claim insurance.

It took two years before his case was heard. All the time he kept using, and a series of lawyers took up his defense. He refused to organize his house, which was chaotic. He had been a wealthy man, and his valuables had started to disappear. He told his sister his twenty-thousand-dollar motor bike had been stolen from his garage, and his twelve-thousand-dollar jet ski was missing. Doors were kicked in, and windows of his home were smashed. It was quite obvious he owed money to his suppliers. His house was full of people, and he refused to let his sister into the house.

His business affairs were a mess. He had debt collectors making threatening calls, and when Andrea tried to answer them they started calling her directly.

All this time Simon was adamant he wouldn't sell his house under any circumstance, and his debts that had become hers accumulated. Not once did he acknowledge his sister for the time and energy she had taken from her life to try and help him. While he was using he did not care, and she was doing all he wanted anyway.

Now he is in prison; he got sentenced to four years. Andrea went to every court appearance and visited him when he was on remand. Now that he has been sentenced, she visits him every week. He is angry; she is sad. He is persuasive; she vacillates on her decisions and has been unable to move forward and tackle all the things she must.

She is exhausted and hurt and now has to prepare his house for sale. She has to pack and store everything he owns, market and sell the house, then deal with all his legal obligations—because now she is financially responsible. She has to sell his million-dollar house, and then she wants to purchase a smaller, more modest and affordable place as a home for him when he comes out.

Andrea is finding it almost impossible to keep up with her job and all the demands on her at present. Her time on weekends is taken up visiting him, and she is dreading telling him the news from the bank: he will be forced into a mortgagee sale within three months. Her parents are ailing; they want to know where he is. She told them he's overseas.

She has tried to explain everything to him, but he's not listening and just yells abuse at her when she visits—and she still goes to visit him because they come from a good family, had wonderful parents, went to the best schools, and always obeyed the law. She is going to wake up from this nightmare any day now, and everything will be all right.

You may see your story among these. Suffice to say, there is no happy ending if you keep using methamphetamine. Apply these tools, and stop now before it is too late. As you have seen from the stories described so far, there is nothing here you don't already know. Everybody is different, and people choose to use the tools in their own way, as you will.

Success is assured if by now you have read the stories—especially if you found one similar to your own—and decided the pain of using methamphetamine outweighs the pleasure. *That is the only thing you have to decide—the tools will guide you with strategies to replace the excuses you have made up until now.*

As a coach, using the tools guides your client's own discovery; it is more effective when it is not seen as a piecemeal, one-off thing but is instead processional, revealing an understanding and awareness to the client that has been previously unknown. The tools help lessen the chaos that is part of the change, making for less knee-jerk reaction and more considerate responses at a time when emotions run high and conflicting influences are at work.

Out of chaos comes order
—UNIVERSAL PRINCIPLE

If you are reading the book to coach another with the tools, do the exercises so you understand the impact and take your own life to a more extraordinary level. These are the same tools I use with my clients from all walks of life who go on to achieve great results in all areas of their lives, both personal and business.

An old Cherokee man was teaching his grandson about life. "A fight is going on inside me," he said to the boy. "It is a terrible fight, and it is between two wolves. One is evil: he is anger, envy, sorrow, regret, greed, arrogance, self-pity, guilt, resentment, inferiority, false pride, superiority, self-doubt, and ego".

"The other is good: he is joy, peace, love, hope, serenity, humility, kindness, benevolence, empathy, generosity, truth, compassion, and faith. This same fight is going on inside you, and in every other person, too"

The child thought about it for a minute and then asked his grandfather, "Which wolf will win?" The old chief replied "The one you feed."

SECTION TWO

Chapter Fifteen
NO ONE TO BLAME

Start the tools with the Circle of Life and work through them in order. There is no time limit; just start. If you are doing this without a coach, you might find it helpful at times to discuss some of the assignments with a friend. Section 3 explains all the tools in greater depth.

Like it or not, you are responsible for the way your life is. Accepting responsibility starts with truly acknowledging the way your life is today, so take a look at the Circle of Life below and, with the center of the circle as zero, draw an arrow to indicate how each area rates out of ten, at the outer circle. For example, if you rate your relationship with family and friends at two, draw your arrow to two out of ten. This is your own self report, your base line, and your rating. Start at the center.

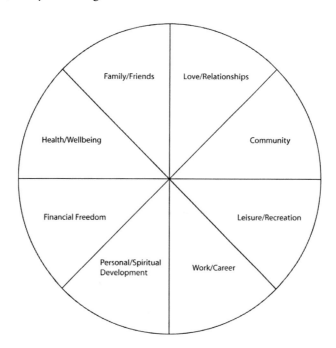

ASSIGNMENT 1
YOUR CIRCLE OF LIFE

As you review your Circle of Life, are there any surprises? Is it what you expected? What does your life look like presently? How satisfied are you right now?

How does it compare with the life you lived before you started using methamphetamine? Be honest. Right at the beginning you may have felt invincible—how long did that last?

What are the costs to of using methamphetamine to you, your family, your friends, the community, your health, and your future?

What will change if you don't? What do you want it to look like? How can that happen?

> *You take your life in your own hands and what*
> *happens- a terrible thing- no one to blame.*
> —ERICA JONG

I have never met anyone yet who, when asked what they wanted for their lives, said anything consciously like "I will get trapped by using drugs, destroy my relationships and my family, lose my business, and jeopardize my children's futures' etc, ad nauseum But how many of you reading this are living any or all of these circumstances? Maybe you know people who are. Perhaps your drug use was a progressive action, or it might have been the only drug you chose. You might mix excessive alcohol along with methamphetamine. Whatever the situation, meth leaves a destructive path that other substances do not. Meth takes away the decent things about you, and so insidiously that you are the last to see what you have become.

But I *have* met many people who, when asked what they want for their wild, precious life, say they don't know, and they end up as the person described in the previous paragraph.

If you don't have a dream, how are you going to have a dream come true?

ASSIGNMENT 2
YOUR VALUES

Values guide and define our choices, which then determine our drive, motivation, and priorities. Values are things like honesty, respect, trust, love, freedom, loyalty, and fairness. You usually learn your values from your first family and from what you observed as a child.

When our values are overridden or contrived, we feel cheated, ripped off, and believe that it is wrong. That is how most people feel when they are robbed, cheated, or violated. People who use methamphetamine rob, cheat, and violate people who don't.

What are your values?

Live so that when your children think of fairness, kindness and integrity they think of you

Chapter Sixteen

Anything You Want

In India, elephants are used for manual labor.

When an elephant is small and weighs approximately two hundred pounds, it is securely tied with a heavy rope. In between jobs, the elephant tries to break away from the rope that limits his freedom. The calf whines, tugs, and tries to chew through the rope but is unable to break free. Finally, the elephant gives up, losing his will. He accepts his circumstances; his spirit is broken.

At the moment the elephant believes there is absolutely no chance to free himself, he has what is known as a defining moment. A defining moment is the exact moment that we adopt or accept a new belief that drastically alters our life. At this point, this new belief becomes a truth, whether it is true or not. Because the brain accepts repetition of thought and deductive reasoning as the truth, the rope will reign as the rule not only in the calf's immediate environment but in his mind as well.

When this belief is firmly embedded in the elephant's mind, he will forever be imprisoned, from now on; in the elephant's mind, any tether will keep him securely confined, and he will not try to break free.

Your self-limiting beliefs are the ones that made you choose pessimism, negativity, cynicism, doubt, fear, and mistrust; it all served a purpose. When you believed you had no other choices, you chose those. *They are instinctive, reflexive and immediate.* If left unchallenged, you will stay trapped in those feelings or take drugs like methamphetamine to alter them.

Self-limiting beliefs cause you to sabotage your success and see your failures as proof of who you are. Change it around.

Self-limiting beliefs started when things were said and done to you when you were a child, when you had less choice to decide that they were not true. Choose how you want it to be.

Defining moments are those moments in your memory that seem most significant, that shaped the way you saw things, that became momentous—some happy, some sad, always defining. This is where you learned the world is a good place, a bad place, or both. That people are good, or bad, or both. You also learned about human nature at work and saw courage and cowardice, love and indifference, hate and acceptance in life. Here you observed resilience, kindness, cruelty, trust, faith, and sadness. None of us live life without experiencing all of it; our lesson is to learn our lesson.

ASSIGNMENT 3
TEN DEFINING MOMENTS IN YOUR LIFE

When you start on a drug that by nature interferes with your ability to feel for others, you certainly stop feeling yourself—you are not living; you are existing.

What were the moments that made you? Can it ever be different? Yes; it's all in your control. Start now by having new defining moments, and make them all motivational and inspiring ones. You do not have to fall in love with your past. If your memories aren't great, change how you saw them; redefine them, reinvent them until they feel okay.

If you want a new future, create a new past.

Don't be like an elephant and live a limited existence. Let your next defining moment be one of freedom, as a choice.

Just thinking makes it so.

ASSIGNMENT 4
SEVEN PEOPLE

Like the moments that played a part in defining who you are, there are people in your life whose actions shaped yours. Who influenced you and how? Name them. Some you know personally, others because they made history or are famous. Why were some situations and the people involved so memorable, and some so forgettable until now? Who would you most like to be like, and why? What are the specific characteristics you notice that makes them special?

As you think about the person you most admire, think about those you least like and the reasons for that dislike. Sometimes the behavior we most despise in others is similar to the side of ourselves we least admire.

Choose your parents or caregivers as a start: what made them who they are?

At any moment I could start being a better person,
but what moment shall I choose?
—ASHLEIGH BRILLIANT

ASSIGNMENT 5
YOUR KNOWLEDGE, SKILLS AND ABILITIES

This is a list of all the things you have accumulated as skills and knowledge. All the things you are capable of and know how to do, such as characteristics and personality traits—anything you are good at. You rock!

The sower may mistake and sow his peas crookedly; the peas
make no mistake, but come up and show his line.
—RALPH WALDO EMERSON

Chapter Seventeenixteen

ANYTHING YOU WANT

ASSIGNMENT 6
THIS IS YOUR LIFE

"This is your life" is your obituary; write it as if you had reached the ripe old age of one hundred and twenty years and were looking back over your life. Tell the story as if you had unlimited financial resources, boundless energy, and were completely supported to achieve anything you could dream—anything!

Here are some questions to prompt you:

- Why did you live for? Why are you alive?
- What do people think of when they think of you?
- What did you leave behind you?
- How do people know you existed?
- What did you do for others?
- If you had your time over again, what would you do?
- How do people know you cared?

Be wild and outrageous, because you have your life back. Imagine if you could determine what would happen for the rest of your life, provided you knew what you wanted and planned with unshakeable faith and determination.

ASSIGNMENT 7
HOW DID I GET HERE?

Take a look back over your life, and admit and acknowledge to yourself the things that you have done up until now—some you can be proud of and some you are not. Ask yourself the hard questions. Don't pretty it up—you did it. Think of ten situations, circumstances, or incidences that, both good and bad, isolate the patterns or strategies you have used or avoided in your life. You cannot keep doing the same things and expect things to be any different.

Ask yourself the following;

- Did I miss important warning signs? Did I ignore warnings? What were they?
- Did I ask what I needed to know?
- When did I lie to myself, and lie to others,
- did I choose the wrong time, place, or people?
- What choices did I offer myself?
- Did I stand up for myself and my rights? What are my rights? Did I impose upon others rights?
- Did I fail to ask for what I wanted? Did I fail to give to give others what they asked for?
- Did I require enough of myself? Have I ever?
- Do I need to stop thinking and acting in certain ways?
- Will thinking and behaving in certain ways make a difference?

Life is cause and effect; you choose the consequence.

We should be careful to get out of an experience only the wisdom that is in it and stop there; lest we be like the cat that sits down on the hot stove lid. She will never sit down on a hot stove lid again – and that is well, but she will never sit down on a cold one again either.

—MARK TWAIN

ASSIGNMENT 8
BLOCKS, RED HERRINGS, AND SABOTAGE

What lies and excuses will you use? I know, calling them lies is pretty harsh, but they are after all.

Now you know the patterns, and strategies, thoughts and behaviors from your past, you have the ability to put into practice new actions- What will stop you?

If you don't tell the truth now, will you ever? Will you ever live to your potential?

Here are some lies, excuses, and reasons you can tell yourself so you can sabotage yourself again and again: No one understands me; that's okay for them to say. It helps me think better. It's not the right time. I didn't have the time. I had the wrong luck/parents/school. I couldn't focus because of the kids and my job; this helps me. It's not as if it's heroin. It's not hurting anyone else; it's my body. It's too hard to give up, and it wasn't my fault. What's the point? I can give up anytime I want; I just don't want to at the moment. It's genetic; I've got an addictive personality.

You have just argued all your self-limiting beliefs, excuses that set you up every time. You have just created a record of the thoughts and beliefs that you will use to sabotage yourself in being free of methamphetamine use.

These are the excuses you will make when things start to change, and it feels difficult and is going to get hard. If you want to keep using them, they will work, and you will not stop using—that's a fact.

Look at them all again, and think of an option for each one instead—then stop using them.

> *There are risks and costs involved in taking a course of action, but not as much as the risks and costs of comfortable inaction.*
> —JOHN F. KENNEDY

ASSIGNMENT 9
CHALLENGE, CHANGE, AND SUCCEED

Frequently we have accepted and adopted thoughts without challenging them. Query your old patterns of thoughts and behaviors. By knowing what these thoughts are, you can ask whether it works to think that way any longer. Then offer yourself alternatives. Holding onto old patterns of thinking and being makes us human. We go with what we know because of two things: it's all we know, and we don't know what to do for things to be different; and simply because we like it that way and don't want it to be different.

But is it working for you for to keep thinking this way?

Chapter Eightteen

LOVE IS THE OLDEST LANGUAGE IN THE WORLD

LOVE RELATIONSHIPS

Love is patient and kind, love does not envy, is not jealous or boastful or proud or rude. It does not demand its own way. It is not irritable, and it keeps no record of being wronged. It does not rejoice about injustice, but rejoices whenever the truth wins out. Love never gives up, never loses faith, is always hopeful, and endures through every circumstance.

—1 CORINTHIANS VS 13

Trust, the foundation for love, is understood and learned in the first year of life. Having a good start means you have a feeling of safety, physical comfort, and a minimal amount of fear and apprehension for the future. When your expectations are low, prison provides this: three meals a day and a bed at night. So for some people, it seems little deterrent when you are messing with methamphetamine—really and truly.

If you learned not to trust, you also learned not to hope. Hope is established when you can plan for the future and know that the world is a good place to live and love. None of these things mean anything when you live with methamphetamine—not for you, your partners, parents, or children. Meth doesn't just affect you, does it?

If you inherited a world that didn't offer you much in the beginning, why should your children? Why perpetuate that? This is the story we tell about drug use being inherited genetically, *the same thoughts that were the drift around you when you grew up are what are inherited.* Change your thoughts. Whether you grew up with drug use around you or not, you learned to accept or refuse them. You see, it's a choice, and it will always be your responsibility.

If you decided drugs were a way of life, for any one of dozens of reasons, then it is no surprise that you will use drugs. The contrary is true: if you swore never to do as others around you, if you have made no association between drugs and good times, then you will not touch them. It all comes down to choices.

There are many reasons you can find to use methamphetamine: it promises you so much, your drug use may have started as wanting a good time, daring convention (your parents have been absolutely opposed, so you did it), you may never have touched other drugs until methamphetamine came along. It is our own thoughts that lead us into trouble, not other people's.

The decision to start using was yours. It is your decision to stop.

That is how simple it is.

So how do you rebuild the trust in yourself, for yourself and others? Start by not using methamphetamine anymore, because using has hurt you on every level of your life, has hurt and betrayed others you used to care for. It costs money you don't have enough of, and it is not going to be a happy ending.

You have got here because you lied and cheated. You don't trust and can't be trusted; to trust and be trusted requires a feeling of physical comfort and a minimal amount of fear and apprehension about the future from yourself and for those around you.

Every time you have told them you will stop then betrayed them, you do damage. Every time your parent, wife, friend, daughter, or son sees you choosing drugs, they know you chose drugs over them. Every time you hurt your children by your behavior, they are learning that they didn't deserve any better, and they will go on to become or marry the person they see in you. You wouldn't want that, would you?

In an experiment, baby monkeys were put in cages with "mother monkeys" made from cloth. They had soft bodies the baby could cuddle, but they were all booby-trapped. The cloth mothers would unexpectedly do a number of cruel things. One shook the baby violently. One had spikes embedded in her chest that would suddenly pop out. When any of the things described happened to them, the babies would cling tighter; if thrust off, they would get up and run right back to their mothers. Get it?

Children who grow up with parents who are not capable spend their life vying for attention; they feel isolated and never good enough. When you use meth, you don't pay attention to your kids or put them first *because you can't.*

You are not good for your children when you use methamphetamine. They love you even when you are horrendous. Children of methamphetamine users cry for their parents, who burn them with cigarettes; put them in dryers because they are bored, and think it's funny; beat them up and kick them like soccer balls; and sexually assault them.

While you are perpetuating abuse of any kind toward your children, you are teaching them their first love lesson. They know it's different and hurts, but they need to think it's right. You are teaching them they deserve to be hurt and disappointed and treated cruelly. You are teaching them that love means pain, and that is what they will look for.

They love you enough to make what you do to them seem right, and they will not argue.

They will replicate their first lessons and either treat others as you have shown them or let others treat them the way you did, and it can take years to discover that it can be different.

Methamphetamine is different to other drugs and makes you cold and cruel and callous toward others, and that means your children suffer. If you are an estranged partner and suspect methamphetamine use where your children live, you aren't protecting them by staying silent and not taking action.. The innocent victims are your children. Don't think it would get worse if you say something. You don't know how bad it will get if you don't say anything.

Stop it before your children get hurt any further.

Forgive yourself and any other person who has done you wrong. Stop your resentment toward others who have more, are more, and have wronged you.

Stop using methamphetamine now or you will never achieve the peace you need to get this monkey off your back.

Your environment has an influence on you. Some situations make you more prone, susceptible, or accepting of what you see or imagine others are doing. Your environment is a key to whether or not you make this easy or hard. That is why you chose the people around you: somehow even if they didn't use, you did around them. Perhaps they didn't know, and since finding out you have no choice now anyway. They will feel angry and disappointed, and cheated, and you will have to go whether you like it or not. If they use with you or continue to use around you, *leave them behind.*

Until you stop using meth, your future is guaranteed to bring you more pain. How many stories are there of people who got involved in smoking meth, started manufacturing methamphetamine to provide their own supply, started supplying others, and stayed using just one more time because the maybe next time they would be lucky, it would pay off, and they would make some money to get rid of their debt? It doesn't seem to work that way, ever.

If love and pain mean the same thing to you—if feeling good means feeling bad—this will not be the first time you have shared an unrequited love. You will no doubt have had a lifetime of pain twisted as love, love twisted as pain. If you are seeking the same pain you learned as love, you have found your drug.

Methamphetamine will inevitably cause you only pain, with no exceptions, and you will never know happiness that is real. **Why are you making that face – it's true!**

You will keep choosing subconsciously to hurt yourself under the guise of feeling good. It may be familiar as love—the elated feeling at first, the confidence you feel that really isn't yours, the false friendships you feel, masquerading as being needed and wanted—until you know better. *Now you do.* So go on—sing a love song to methamphetamine, the lying lady. *"I'll love you till the day I die. I can't live without you. You are everything to me ..."*

DRUGS DO NOT LOVE YOU

Test your love affair with methamphetamine and the friends who provide it to you. When you can't afford it, you are expected to steal, beg, or cheat to pay for it, or those friends of yours will break your legs—because they don't really love you! Instead, try saying to yourself, "You are more than this will ever be," and fall in love with yourself.

> *When I speak of love, I am not speaking of some sentimental or weak response. I am speaking of that force which all of the great religions have seen as the supreme unifying principle of life. Love is somehow the key that unlocks the door which leads to ultimate reality.*
> —MARTIN LUTHER KING, JR.

HOW TO LOVE YOURSELF

- Stop doing methamphetamine, now and forever.
- Decide you are worthy of giving and receiving love by telling yourself a love story with a new beginning and different ending to the one you are playing out, where you are the star.
- Forgive yourself and others who have harmed you.
- Choose the people you spend time with (the ones who know how to care) and the things you spend your time doing.
- Start to care for yourself and others.
- Make right what you can, immediately.
- Help someone else stop using methamphetamine; this will keep you strong in your own conviction.

I thought I would include some questions to gauge whether the relationship you are currently in is healthy. If you are single right now, this will help in your next choice. The same questions apply to relationships with your family and friends. You might discover you are so wounded that you are not capable of being all you need to be to maintain a relationship on an intimate level.

It's comforting to be in a relationship that works, and one that doesn't can be just as satisfying, because your partner can take the blame, your partner can become the reason why it got too hard to achieve freedom, and the heat's off you. So, think carefully about whether this will hurt or heal you or your partner.

You may be reading this as the partner/victim of a user, and you don't use yourself and didn't know about his or her use. You will go through a myriad of emotions, as no doubt you have already. You will accuse yourself of being stupid, naive, and gullible. You're forgetting the person you know has become a master of deceit and is incapable of loving himself or herself, let alone you, the children, or his or her parents while using methamphetamine. You may be naive but not stupid.

You deserve better. Now you know. With no exceptions, they can choose to stop, right now.

You cannot do it for them, and they are not allowed to blame you or direct their anger at you.

You may be married with a family, and your partner may be the income earner. The more responsibility you have toward each other makes it even more vital that you get this right, so if must be apart, you must.

ASSIGNMENT 10
LOVE WILL SET YOU FREE

This assignment will help you to establish whether your existing relationship is healthy and can last your changes, or whether it needs to be part of the change. Either way, love for yourself will set you free.

- What am I getting out of this relationship?
- How is this benefiting my life right now? Is this love?
- How am I growing and becoming a better person as a result of this relationship?
- Do I feel safe, respected, and loved, even now?
- Are my new needs being met—my emotional, physical, mental, and spiritual needs?
- Can I talk openly, without feeling foolish or stupid
- Is he/she faithful?
- Do I feel happy and fulfilled more than I feel unhappy or frustrated? Do I feel guilty or anxious around this person?
- Does this relationship allow me to be true to myself now that I am free—my values, beliefs, and spirit?

- Do we have similar life goals and dreams now that I don't use methamphetamine?
- If my best friend were in this relationship, what would I tell her/him to do?
- If this relationship were to end, would I truly be sad about losing her/him, or sad that she/he is not the person I wanted her/him to be?

Let a partner go if he or she doesn't or can't meet your new needs. Right now, what are they? *After a drug-free environment, finding yourself is the most important thing.* If your current partner is drug free like you, and neither of you will tempt the other, there is strength in staying together, but not if he or she is still using.

> *Most of us remain strangers to ourselves, hiding who we are,*
> *and ask other strangers, hiding who they are, to love us.*
>
> —LEO BUSCAGLIA

If they truly want the best for you, they will do what is best for you and will wait until things get better for you both.

Someone will come into your life who is worthy, when you are worthy and can love you the way you deserve to be loved, when you can signal that you are ready. (But the right person can't find you if you're with the wrong person!)

The reality is, no matter how hard you try, you can't have a drama-free relationship if you're with the wrong person—or are the wrong person.

You don't need any more drama; that's the truth.

And remember, the same questions in the previous assignment apply to you. Your partner, family, and friends are entitled to only the best from you. Do the assignment again from the other person's point of view.

You Are More Than This Will Ever Be

And in the end, the love you get is equal to the love you gave.
—THE BEATLES

Learning to love yourself again means you will not have to distort reality any longer. Love does not mean cruel, callous, and unkind behavior. Ask successful people what they do, read about them, make plans to spend your time doing other things instead, and turn your focus to making right what you can for others.

There are going to be times when nothing feels comfortable; you feel alienated and think that you don't fit in. It's better than being a meth head and having a life that will spiral completely out of control. Someone will help if you ask. Ask me if you feel there is no one who cares enough. **e**mail me at ultimatecoach@xtra.co.nz **– I'm serious.**

Love makes the world go 'round.
—THE BEATLES

Our deepest fear is not that we are inadequate, rather that we are powerful beyond measure! It is our light not our darkness, that frightens us. We ask ourselves, who am I to be brilliant, happy, beautiful, talented and strong? Who are you not to be, you are a child of God, it is not enlightened to shrink in front of others. We were born to manifest the glory that is within us, it's not just in some of us, it is in every one of us. As we let our own light shine we unconsciously give others permission to do the same, as we liberate ourselves from fear, our presence automatically liberates others!

—MARIANNE WILLIAMSON

Methamphetamine is nothing compared to who you will find inside yourself again.

Being deeply loved by someone gives you strength, while loving someone deeply gives you courage.
—LAO TZU

Chapter Nineteen

FAMILY AND FRIENDS

Ike aku, Ike ma, kokua aku kokua mai; pei ho la ka nohona ohana. Recognize others, be recognized, help others, be helped; such is the family relationship. Give and take is the natural process of family. Value and respect your family and friends. Recognize your value in a family, and you recognize your value in society.
—THE LITTLE BOOK OF ALOHA

Friends and family can be separated, and as the old saying goes, you can choose your friends, but you can't choose your family. The only thing to consider right now is, *are you able to manage the changes living where you are?*

It is all up to you; there's no one to blame, lay excuses, on or manipulate any longer, because you have to become the change you want for your life. How much do you want it?

The same applies to the family—it may have been convenient for you to be the family bad boy or bad girl.

Because of you, others in your family may appear more saintly, virtuous, and long–suffering, and because they want it to stay that way, they may not be ready for you as a whole person. If their behavior toward you is the same, if they are not prepared for things to be different, then you will have to prove it to them: you don't fit anymore in a family system that enjoyed you more as a drug user, and you will have to leave to come back.

As their family member, you have to choose to believe them when they say they are free and will not use again. When they stop using, their feelings for others return, and they unfreeze. This can be overwhelming because it will remind you how bad things got to get here now.

The implications of their using may be coming to light for the first time, and the consequences may be too much for you to live with. As a family member, doing the exercises in this book will give you a clearer picture of your life today and how you would like it to be tomorrow.

A scar is easily wounded.
—TSONGA TRIBE SAYING

If your relationships are still intact, the damage you caused is not too great, you are surrounded by support, and you can avoid any old contacts, stay where you are.

If you can stay where you are without causing any more pain and distress than you already have to yourself and your family, then set up a new code of ethics and behavior that you all agree to and adhere to it.

This is not easy to do; patterns are automatic, and they have gone unchallenged up until now. *You are responsible for challenging them; no one else will.*

Sometimes you don't get the choice, and you need to move. Some reasons to move are other people are using around you, or you have stolen or cheated or behaved violently and are no longer welcome. It is ironic that while you get better, those closest to you will sometimes get bent out of shape—they have learned to live with your irrational, unreliable behavior. They know and understand that because they have become used to it; they know what to expect from you, and they know what not to expect too.

You may have learned to live with theirs, too—that's one reason you might think you take drugs. It hasn't worked though, has it?

As being human, we get trapped into patterns, and it will tempt you to continue using. Maybe staying at your parents or family home will ensure the same good food, lifestyle, and cash—so why change? This is what you know.

Most family and friends who aren't users themselves say you have come back; they know you again the moment you decide to. Family and friends who used with you know when it changes too; they will not like it.

Again, you may ironically be the primary caregiver or provider for your husband, wife, or children and need to stay where you are; then you must change everything else around you. Stop certain habitual responses and behaviors, and start new ones. It is as simple as filling your day differently, practicing stress management techniques, planning a little further in your life, and finding ways that you feel rewarded and recognized for the things you are achieving daily. Pull your weight; start contributing to life in the family.

If you are doing this on your own and have told nobody of your use, good for you, but it will be easier if you find someone you can trust enough to support you all the way. If you don't know anybody around you who can do that, then find someone—an old friend, a member of your extended family, whoever. If you don't ask around, you are not giving anybody else the opportunity to help you.

This is where things are complex and can be more difficult, because you will need to become the change you want to see. You will have to stop manipulating others to get your way. You will have to change your lifestyle and daily habits. You will have to stop seeing friends that use drugs and find a job if you don't already have one.

You have set patterns in your relationships; you can wheedle and inveigle your way, and it's worked so far. *What will be different if you are not?* These are things to consider if you are staying where you are.

Staying with people who let you have your way (unwittingly or not) will keep you using and lying about it. There are ways to make it work, but everyone you live with needs to make changes to how they treat you and how you treat them, and clear rules are needed so that if they are breached, you know what to do. As a reminder, we are talking about a drug that destroys families. If that isn't clear to you, leave them now; it will be better for them. There cannot be room for any further tolerance.

If you want freedom from drug use, think you have to stay because of circumstances, and live with another user in the house, you just have to be a little more determined and vigilant, and make a decision that does not allow for mistakes. You have to go, even if only temporarily. If you can't, you must.

You Are More Than This Will Ever Be

Lie down with a dog and you wake up with fleas.
Like attracts like—a rule of physics!

If the people around you doubt you, either face up to them or go and live somewhere else. It helps to have people on your side. Unless they change with you, up until now, these people have let you get away with nothing but trouble, and they may be nothing but trouble. *If they aren't prepared to expect something different from you, you may be tempted not to.*

If you are asking someone to run with you, you better be
prepared to sprint yourself.

RULES FOR LIVING WITH YOUR FAMILY

- Ask someone to run with you.
- Do not manipulate, lie, and cheat your family and friends anymore.
- Eat, sleep, and live family routines, if they are regular and don't include methamphetamine.
- Move if they do use—or be prepared for the fight of your life.
- Start to show how you can care for others, offer help, and start being useful.
- Don't give in—it won't always be as hard as this.

Each one of us who travels further than the obstacles will
know a different kind of life from that time on.
—J. STONE

RULES WITH FRIENDS

- Absolutely no methamphetamine use around you.

Right now, somebody is thinking of you, caring about you, missing you, wanting to talk to you, be with you, and hoping you aren't in trouble. Someone is thankful for the support you have provided, wants to hold your hand, hopes everything will turn out all right, wants you to be happy, wants you to find him or her, is celebrating your success, wants to give you a gift, thinks you are a gift, loves you, admires your strength, is thinking of you and smiling, and wants to be your shoulder to cry on.

Chapter Twenty

WHAT KIND OF DEAL?

ASSIGNMENT 11
PROMISES, PROMISES

I, (user name here) promise to myself and commit to you (your lover, friend or family members names here) to stop using methamphetamine without any more excuses, lies or deceit, now I have all the tools and strategies to achieve complete freedom.

I, (user name here), promise not to harm you physically, (your lover, friend, or family member here) or blame you while I am recovering. If I frighten you, lie, steal or cheat you or the children I must go, immediately.

I, (user name here), will not use, supply, or manufacture methamphetamine again. If I do, I must go, because while I can ruin my life on my own, I don't need to ruin yours any longer.

Your signature here _____

Date _____

Don't think twice- this is what it takes, and now you have some rules to live by.

We ought to remember that we are not the only ones to find ourselves at an apparent impasse. Just as a kite rises against the wind, even the worst of troubles can strengthen us. As thousands before us have met the identical fate and mastered it, so can we.
—DR. R BRANSCH

Keep a green tree in your heart, and perhaps the singing bird will come.
—CHINESE PROVERB

Chapter Twenty-one

It'll Be Tough for a Bit

WORK AND CAREER

People think responsibility is hard to bear. It's not. I think sometimes it is the absence of responsibility that is hard to bear.
—Henry Kissinger

You might have gotten this far without anyone knowing, if you haven't committed any crimes like theft, think it is up to you, and think it's okay not to tell anyone.

One of the stories I hear more and more is in regard to adult sons or daughters who work in family businesses. In each case, the use has become extensive, and over time money, often a large amount, has been stolen, and it will go on—so stop it!

Generally they have held a responsible position and managed to escape the auditing or other checks. Then they get found out. It is frequently not believed at first. How could they breach their positions of trust and power this way? *That's easy: the same way they have done it in every other aspect of their lives!* Then comes the difficult legal process to extradite them, again at a cost to the family that is more than financial.

The family feels the shame and the embarrassment to their reputation, taken on both professionally and personally, and often the family does not take the user to court, so he or she never gets the justice he or she is due.

The precedent owners are usually elderly and expecting to reap the rewards of their own efforts when suddenly they find themselves fighting to redeem the standing they had in the business community, all while their families fall apart.

If you are a victim to fraud of any kind, report it as you would any theft. Stop making excuses; you are not saving your son, daughter, or partner from anything by ignoring it—you are condoning it.

Permissive attitudes will lead you to always crave, never be completely free, they will keep you in contact with people who use drugs, and you will keep associating drugs with friends—no one wants to feel lonely, do they? Why would you stop under those circumstances?

If you are working with other users, stop associating with them. This is almost impossible if they are your boss or you have been supplying to workmates, so get a new job. I suggest getting a job where you know there is regular drug testing; that'll keep you on your toes.

There is sometimes fallout if you are caught at work and stay on in employment. If your workmates and colleagues find out, they will use it against you, and you will have to defend yourself. If you get caught by your employer and are offered the opportunity to stay, other employees may resent the opportunity you have been given.

Not everybody will be on your side; they will not think you are a hero, will not believe you can give up, and will use the knowledge they have about you against you every time you do anything. If they use and didn't get caught, they will try to start you using again and will never trust you if you don't.

It'll be tough for a bit.

Chapter Twenty-two
WHAT WOULD YOU RATHER BELIEVE?

HEALTH AND WELLBEING

Mai ka piko o ke po'o a ka poli o ka wawae a la'a ma na kihi eha o ke kino. From the crown of the head, to the soles of the feet, and the four corners of the body.
—THE LITTLE BOOK OF ALOHA

The medical field has so much variation on the effects of methamphetamine use, it doesn't make any sense. Some research will assure you the residual chemical dependence will linger for two years. Other learned comment will assure you that you will crave for five years, two months, or two weeks. *What about choosing two hours—what would you rather believe?*

Haven't you heard stories of people defying medical odds? Make your story of immediately nailing methamphetamine use on its head one of those.

Think of a cat being caught in a corner by a dog, its eyes wide and terrified, its fur on end making them twice the size. That's the state you have put yourself into every time you smoke methamphetamine. Meth is a central nervous system stimulant, and the first rush of excitement leaves a residue of anxiety, fear, and paranoia. That's how it works. Meth causes a fight-or-flight response: to prepare you for a fight you must get angry; to run, you must be suspicious. So when the initial rush is done, that's what you get left with— you are still angry and suspicious.

ASSIGNMENT 12
HEALTH AND WELLBEING SELF-EVALUATION

Please answer the following:

- Is good physical health of major importance to me? Are my habits consistent with good health? Am I in good health now? Do I need medical attention at this time?

- Are my attitudes toward my own health in my long-term interests?
- Have I had a complete physical check up in the last two years? Have I seen my dentist in the last year?
- Do I know the signs of mental and emotional stress? Do I respond appropriately to these signs?
- Is my energy level always sufficient for the work I am doing? Do I need to review my diet? How is my mental attitude to the work I do?
- Does my daily routine include any physical exercise? Do I frequently work long hours without a rest? Do I miss meals or eat on the run?
- How do I relax? What do I do for fun?
- Do I get as much exercise as I need? Do I get the right kind of exercise?
- What nutritional habits do I have? Do I eat a balanced, optimum diet?

Health is more than the absence of sickness. Health is the presence of aliveness, energy, and joy. You don't have to be sick to get better. Health does not just refer to the body; health is mind, emotions, the whole person.

You don't get to choose when you die; you do, however, get to choose how to live!

—JOAN BAEZ

ASSIGNMENT 13
STRESS CHECK

Using methamphetamine has stressed your mind, body, and spirit. It is no longer your first escape when things get tough, so complete the following questions and design a new strategy for you to rely on.

What are the significant consequences of stress in the following areas? Please answer the following questions:

- How does stress affect your physical, emotional, and mental states? What are your warnings?

- How do you react emotionally when you are stressed? How do you feel when you are stressed?
- How do you cope mentally? What do you think and say to ease or minimize your levels of stress?
- When you are stressed, lonely, happy, or sad; what will you do instead of using methamphetamine? Name three things.

Getting healthy is essential to getting better and not using. As your body heals, so too will your mind; as your mind clears, so too will your body. Methamphetamine stresses every organ in your body. Your body has been under attack and in a state of high alert—every time you smoked, every cell in your body has been affected by poison, your heart has had to work overtime, and your nerves are shot!

Following are different things you can do to manage your health and well-being.

You have heard them all before. Now you know you must do something. You have stressed every organ in your body—your liver, heart, kidneys, and brain.

You are on the verge of getting your life back. Awesome!

Your body's chemical balance has been messed with. Methamphetamine interferes with your own natural ability to communicate messages to itself, to hormones like insulin, and to neurotransmitters such as serotonin and dopamine (which make you feel good). This insulin imbalance will lead to the blood-sugar blues (which is why you crave sugar) and depression because of a shortage of serotonin. Remember, methamphetamine messes with your mind.

Detoxify your body. All drugs have toxic effects on the body, so detoxing is essential. Cleansing allows your body to clear out defective and diseased cells and chemical residue. As cells repair and regenerate, your immunity, resistance to disease, and vitality increase.

Sleep is restorative and reparative. If you exercise and eat well, you should be tired at night. When you sleep, your subconscious sifts through and deals with problems. When you get adequate sleep, you manufacture growth hormone, which helps you stay young and strong.

You will need to start taking Omega 3, which contains essential fatty acids. They make up the membranes of every cell in your body and control what is flowing in and out of them—oxygen, viruses, waste, and fluids. Omega 3 is needed for our brain cells, eyes, adrenal glands, and nerves. Yours are shot—you need this!

Drink water. You know this. Your cells need water to stay energized and detox ASAP.

Get lots of light. You have turned your body clock inside out by staying up all night. Now you need to get as much natural light as possible to help your moods and maintain your hormonal balance. Apart from obvious other benefits, being awake during the day means you can work and socialize.

Deep breathing oxygenates your cells, stops brain fog, and helps you to concentrate. First thing in the morning, and any time you feel you are lagging in energy, breathe deeply.

Exercise, walk, run, jog, jump, and smile. You're doing good.

Relaxation—that's both being still and actively doing things that give you a feeling of satisfaction. Relaxing doesn't include staring at the TV for hours. Start reading again—something inspirational or interesting. Doing something physical is relaxing, as long as it is not related to drugs, people you know who take or sell drugs, or anywhere drugs will be involved. Yes, you have to start all over again.

Pray or meditate. Take time to be silent, grateful, and expectant. You got your life back again. See the end of this section for instructions on how to meditate and a prayer.

Start eating well. The fresher the better: fruits, nuts, and vegetables are best for you right now. Stay away from sugar, sugar drinks, white bread, cakes, and processed food. I know that sounds easy—it is. Just try it and feel the difference.

Don't drink alcohol or smoke dope. It's a depressant, and you don't need any more of that

Make time. Don't use the excuse you haven't got time. Do a time inventory and find some, and accept that you have just wasted a lifetime and will continue to do so if this recovery doesn't work.

Start to laugh and love again. Be grateful for what you have, and now that you are making smart decisions, be grateful for what the future will bring you and the others who rely on you.

> *When eating, be mindful of eating; when walking, be mindful*
> *of walking; when smiling, be mindful of smiling.*
> —BUDDHA

One thing at a time; one day at a time. You're doing great!

ASSIGNMENT 14
AN ACCOUNT OF MY LIFE

If you are going to view your life from a position of accountability, a good place to begin is to reevaluate the history where you cast yourself as a recipient of and victim of circumstance. Keep it real; remember, there will always be people who are luckier, clever, and smarter than you. Maybe you didn't take advantage of the things you did have going for you—yet!

> *When you get into a tight place and everything goes against you till it*
> *seems as though you could not hang on a minute longer, never give up*
> *then, for that is just the place and time that the tide will turn.*
> —HARRIET BEECHER STOWE

ASSIGNMENT 15
RESULTS IN MY LIFE SO FAR

Measuring success or failure purely as a function of results means taking a hard-nosed, bottom-lined approach to self-evaluation. You might as well do it this way; after all, this is how you are measured by others. This is a baseline from which to start again, so include material results as well as accomplishments in anything you can recall that makes you proud.

ASSIGNMENT 16
BE GRATEFUL FOR WHAT YOU'VE GOT

You're alive and getting stronger. There is a lot to be grateful for. Any resentment you may still have eases when you are grateful for what you have now. You're alive, and your life is on track again. That's something to be grateful for.

Make a list of everything in your life that you have achieved. Mention things you have admired about yourself and the good things others have done in your life. The idea is to be grateful for the things that make every day worth living. Start with the simple things you can appreciate, like the sun coming up every day. Your list will surprise you.

You know things are looking better when you start to be grateful for the situations in your life that used to cause you pain. Make your list, and read it every day, morning and night. Sweet dreams!

Chapter Twenty-three

MONEY: ANOTHER PART OF THE PUZZLE

FINANCIAL FREEDOM

Knowledge is king! Getting back on track financially means knowing where your money went and acts as a reminder that you have paid a big price. This is just one perspective, and this is one way of getting control back over your life.

It is important to be honest about what you did and how you did it to pay the cost of the drugs you used. You need to see how much your behavior has cost you and your family, how opportunities that passed you by, how your reputation has been affected. In finances alone now, you are starting to count the costs.

You might have been selling and profiting up until now. By making the decision not to use anymore, you may have had to give up a lifestyle you afforded through others' misery—good thing you got out.

You may have to fess up to theft, cashing checks, using credit cards that didn't belong to you, and helping yourself to the joint account pretending you were using the money for other things, like school fees for the kids, council rates, or mortgage payments. Bring it out into the cold, hard day. By facing up to it, you can start to make amends and make it better.

There may be financial misery in front of you, stuff you wanted to avoid previously. It didn't go away, and it won't. Smoking methamphetamine helped you forget, but it can only get worse. Meth made you feel nothing else mattered—but it does. The sooner you tell the truth about all aspects of your life, the sooner your life can get better. As part of your discovery, you need to address any of the damage you have done, and it will get better.

It will be a brand-new start, and frequently after a crash, you get back into life with a vengeance. How many times do you hear people say it was through adversity that they got a new start and never looked back?

Take this Financial Health Check. Comment on each statement; you may be surprised that you adopted ways of thinking that only need challenging for things to change forever.

ASSIGNMENT 17
MY FINANCIAL HEALTH CHECK

- What does money mean to me?
- How does not having money affect my life?
- How does having money impact on my life?
- What did money mean to my parents? Is that true?
- I know where my money goes.
- I balance my bank statement every month.
- I always pay my bills on time.
- I am responsible for my financial circumstances.
- I live debt free.
- I save money consistently.
- I don't depend on lotto to fund my financial future.
- I have a long-term financial plan that supports my present and future goals.
- I am financially secure; I don't worry about money.
- I share my wealth with others.
- I pay my credit cards in full each month.
- I pay my taxes on time.
- I have a financial adviser/accountant/coach who knows my goals.
- I know what I need to do to start to make it better.

How did you do? What is your story about money? Becoming honest about your financial situation is the first step. Inaction will keep you a victim to external forces, stress you out, and make this all so much harder.

As with anything you need to cope with currently, start by taking simple steps and ask for help if you need it. Staying free from using methamphetamine is the highest priority. You must address your financial situation, and while it may be hard and a savage reminder of what you have lost, it won't change by ignoring it.

To organize your finances, start by drawing up a schedule of your financial incoming and outgoing. Include all your living expenses and any debt you may have, and tally up the amounts. You might need to find a volunteer through Citizens Advice or social services or Salvation Army to help you manage your budget.

You may need help with your tax returns, child support, or debt you have accumulated. If you are in trouble financially, it will not go away. Get whatever help you need as soon as possible. Your recovery should not be threatened over money troubles; they can be dealt with.

You might still owe money to the person who was supplying your drugs at this point. In my experience you will have to honor your debt, or you may find yourself in too deep. They will not make it easy for you; they just saw their income and own supply threatened. They might ring you for months—if that is all, you are lucky. Gangs who have multimillion-dollar stakes in this game mean business—you knew that from the beginning—and they will do whatever it takes to get it. It is not in their best interest to lose a regular—it is in yours, though. Pay them their money and change your phone number.

The hen of a poor person does not lay eggs, and even if she lays eggs,
she never hatches, and if she hatches, she never rears the chicks,
and when she rears, the chicks are taken by the hawk.
—SWAHILI SAYING

Like everything, just keep going one step at a time, and it will get better.

Chapter Twenty-four

YOU ARE A STAR

PERSONAL AND SPIRITUAL DEVELOPMENT

Fear knocked on the door; faith answered—there was no one there.
—THE SOPRANOS

Personal and spiritual development is understood differently by each of us. One of the consequences of choosing to grow emotionally and mentally means you will find courage and strength in yourself and others.

Having faith offers you comfort and a feeling that you are not alone, that you are part of a majestic universe, and it promises forgiveness. Get some now! There are many religions, doctrines, philosophies, and beliefs you can adopt. Religion is an organized path toward spirituality. Start somewhere; find a quiet place; and ask, read about, or visit places people go to worship. You find good people in these places; surround yourself with them.

If anything, I hope that now you are this far you have begun to be honest with yourself. What you have done is cause other people pain—the people you have hurt most are usually the people closest to you. You may have been violent and physically hurt others, cheated on your partner, and lied. You have been unreliable, selfish, and deceitful. So what now? You cannot change the things you have done, or turn back the clock. What is done is done; the only thing you can do now is stop using methamphetamine, forgive yourself, and make things better whenever you can.

No matter what happens next, forgiving yourself is vital. It doesn't mean you can abscond from your responsibility or minimize your wrongdoings, but forgiving yourself will give you freedom to make things better.

If you stay trapped and guilty, you will look for reasons to feed your increasing guilt, anxiety, and self-loathing, and they will come! The next bit is easy: *if you don't forgive yourself, you will start using again* because you are not worthy, and who would care anyway—that is how you are thinking after all. Forgiving yourself is so critical to ending your reliance on methamphetamine.

Unforgiveness toward yourself and others means you are letting them and the past dictate your today and tomorrow, leaving a legacy your children will inherit.

Forgiving yourself involves deepening your understanding of you in the world. It leads to greater spiritual awareness, whatever that means to you. It helps to spend time with people who are also seeking answers, or people who have found answers that make them stronger and more trusting in life.

When you meditate, your brain's electrical activity is calmed through an increase in brain waves associated with deep relaxation. By meditating, you slow your body's metabolic rate down, which that leads to more efficient oxygen consumption, and when you are detoxing, this helps! Meditation decreases your blood pressure and pulse rate, and you feel more relaxed and less stressed. There is a prayer and a meditation at the end of this section.

Protect yourself from people who don't speak positively. Love yourself. Start by saying only positive things to yourself, your family, and your friends. Listen to how you are speaking to yourself. Stop the cruel things you say, and use positive affirmations until you believe them yourself. You may as well—it doesn't take any more effort.

Don't look for trouble and tempt fate. Leave your old contacts alone—get better yourself. It will not happen if you hang around with users. You don't have the strength; you have already proved that.

Look after yourself. Look after your heart, and don't be reckless with anybody else's heart. Stay away from people who confuse you right now. Sometimes people aren't always honest in their intentions—you know that.

If you owe money, get a job, make arrangements to pay it back, and do! Why does that matter? Because how can you forgive someone who is still ripping off other people? Gget a job anyway.

*The whole purpose of religion is to facilitate love, compassion,
patience, tolerance, humility, and forgiveness.*

—Dalai Lama

ASSIGNMENT 18
AN EXERCISE IN FORGIVENESS

Forgiving yourself and others is essential; by now you know that.

Try the following exercise:

Clench your fist tightly, and hold it. Keep holding it. After just a few minutes, your nails are digging into your palm; it's uncomfortable and irritating, and it hurts. Keep holding tightly.

Try and do or think of something else while you are still holding tightly. It's quite distracting, isn't it? It's hard to think of anything else when you are uncomfortable and preoccupied. Keep holding; after the initial pain, you go numb.

Keep your fist squeezed tightly for at least another ten minutes, then try and let go, just a little at a time, like we do when we are still not really prepared to let go completely. It's impossible when your fingers are so cramped that they can't move. The only way to free your fingers and stop the pain is to throw your hand out, spreading your fingers, once and for all. Let it all go at once. So, will you?

Forgive, but don't forget.

Chapter Twenty-five

LIVE IN HARMONY

Ho'omoe wai kahi ke kao'o- Let's all travel together like water flowing in the same direction. Live in harmony with other people and the world around you; live in harmony with your own beliefs and aspirations.

—THE LITTLE BOOK OF ALOHA

COMMUNITY

ASSIGNMENT 19
YOU AND YOUR COMMUNITY

- Who do you define as community?
- Why are you linked?
- What do you do for your community?
- Who have you harmed?
- How would your community help you?
- How can you help the community you are part of?

Your answers will include contacts you lost as your involvement in using escalated and your previous community was pushed further away. That may have included your children's school friends and parents, your wider family, work colleagues, sports teams—anything you shared interest in before the drug that took anything worthwhile away. How easy will it be to get it all back? It may be possible; if not, start again. You may only have known the friends that surrounded you as a user. Start again.

Getting better means you have to relinquish things, places, and people. It's not the end of the world—not getting better is, though.

You must understand the whole of life and not just one little part of it. That is why you must read, that is why you must look at the stars, and that is why you must sing and dance, and write poems and suffer; and understand, for all that is life.
—KRISHNAMURTI

LEISURE AND RECREATION

You are going to have more time now, and you will probably feel a myriad of emotions: confused and lonely at first. And immediately before it feels better, others will be relieved, excited, and free. Whatever you are feeling, enjoying being alive is a good start. Do simple things, and include plenty of exercise, fresh air, and time alone to consider the changes you have made.

You are not seeing any of your friends that still use meth anymore. Maybe because you have burned your friends who don't use methamphetamine, they don't want you around anymore. Life will get better.

It is really important that you start to enjoy living again. Do all you can to make amends—that is all you can do—and spend time every day doing something that rewards you and that you enjoy doing.

As a family person, you have taken time from your family. Maybe you have lost the opportunity to see your children. Maybe, as with other family members, your children have suffered the shame of your drug using by seeing you go to jail, destroy friendships, and disappoint them. It's you who has to make amends—stop using, no more exceptions. Stop it.

Children are pretty forgiving. What can you do to give them back their childhood? Let them be innocent again; they currently worry for you, and for them. Jail seems so ineffective here; a bunch of people who have done similar things become your reference, and we know that you become like the five people you spend time with. Choose as well as you can.

If you are not in jail and have access to your children, play with and talk to them—it's their right. If their other parent is in a new relationship getting his or her life back, don't make it any harder than it already is. Your children and their happiness matter more than any more of your self-indulgent choices. Your kids just want it to be normal. You don't have to try too hard; just spend time with them and do simple things. Start acting like a decent parent, and start putting them and their needs before you.

It's the same thing with your teenagers: give them time. What will you say if/ when you catch your teenager doing drugs? Talk to them; it's never too late. That may seem to be beyond your reach, but they may not be. They may have slipped your grasp, and while you say they don't listen to a thing you are saying, they watch everything you do. Watch what you do.

What are you, if not a great example that methamphetamine took more than it ever offered you. Kids who are informed make better choices, so tell them about the bad times (within reason). There were plenty of them. Then show them by your actions that you do not do that stuff anymore. Show them the options you have now, and the choices you make now. Love them. Love yourself.

A scorpion came up to a frog sitting by a fast flowing river. He told the frog he was desperate to get to the other side, adding he couldn't swim because he was a scorpion, and he asked if the frog would give him a ride on his back.

The frog said, "You're a scorpion, and scorpions sting frogs."

"But why would I do that?" answered the scorpion. "I want to get to the other side." So the frog agreed and told the scorpion to get on his back.

When they were almost halfway across, the scorpion stung the frog. "But why did you sting me? Now we will both drown."

"Because," said the scorpion, "I'm a scorpion, and scorpions sting frogs"

No surprises, are there?

Start to be responsible for every action, every thought, and all your behavior. This is where you need a friend who cares enough to see you through in spite of what you may have done, so deepen your spiritual awareness and ask for the help and understanding you need. Just ask.

The reason you used meth was it promised so much: elation, success, charisma, and invincibility. The good news is this is all naturally occurring ... when you get it right again. Meth may promise to be a shortcut to how people who are successful live, but as you have found out, meth offers only a temporary parody that you are calling your life.

The feeling you are trying to emulate is a result of living a life of courage. What does that make you? How are you living now? How can you live so you are who you would like to be?

> *The world is conspiring for you.*
> —CONSPIRACY THEORY

Success can be defined as many things; each of us has our own perspective on what success means. If you stop using meth, what will that look like to you? All your friends will change. How will it be to have to start over again, which is inevitable? While you are using, these people are not your friends, and you are not theirs. Friends don't do this to each other.

One of the Hawaiian greetings is to say "pehea kou piko," which means how is your spirit?

How is your spirit?

Chapter Twenty-six
THE WAY YOU DO THE THINGS YOU DO

ASSIGNMENT 20
CHARACTERISTICS OF SUCCESSFUL PEOPLE

Rate yourself

The following are considered to be some of the skills and characteristics of successful people. Rate yourself from one to ten on each of these behaviors: Confidence, optimism, strength, passionate, ability to love, patience, consistency, flexibility in thinking, accepting yourself and others, generosity, focused ambitious, action with integrity, enthusiasm, imagination, decisiveness, kindness, motivational, ability to see the best in others.

So how did you rate?

Eighty percent of the success achieved by star performers in all walks of life and business is attributed to emotional competency. You may need to develop yours.

Achieving success means developing the right combination of positive attitudes, mind-sets, beliefs, emotions, and habits, as well as choosing the most resourceful skills, knowledge, and behaviors.

Whatever the difference is between where you rate yourself today and where you would like to be, it is up to you.

Now you have a target, more than a promise, and it's cheaper because it doesn't involve methamphetamine.

ASSIGNMENT 21
ATTITUDE IS EVERYTHING

Review the following questions:

*   How is your attitude?

- What does living successfully mean to you now?
- What are your three strengths?
- What are your three weakest behaviors?
- What will you develop for this challenge?
- How?

You have one wild and precious life—what are you doing with yours?

There were two brothers. Both grew up with the same parents, both had the same teachers and influences on their life, and each gained notoriety for very different reasons. Their father was bad; he cheated and was in and out of jail, an irresponsible drunk. One of the brothers studied hard, achieved much, earned respect, married, had children, worked hard in his community, and become a bastion of his society. The other brother left school before he gained any qualifications, spent time in jail for crimes he committed, drank, got caught dealing drugs, and had nothing.

The extremities of their lives were such that a journalist interviewed them. His question was obvious: "How could two sons of the same father have such different lives?"

The first son replied, "With a father like mine, how could it be any different?" When the reporter asked the second son the same question, he also said, "With a father like mine, how could it be any different?

If you want better or different, you need to make changes immediately, irrevocably and with no exceptions.

I want my dreams back. I've been a slave to you; you've got a hold on me.
—COMMON SENTIMENT SHARED BY METH USERS

Chapter Twenty-seven
Goal Setting

The futures so bright, I gotta wear shades.
—'80s SONG BY TIMBUK 3

WHY SET GOALS

Methamphetamine steals. As a user, you have lost friends, family, money and possessions, to say nothing of your pride, respect, and ability to trust and be trusted. Goals clarify your choices; you become more reliable, and small accomplishments are better than none. Setting goalsThis tracks the decisions and choices you make and lets other people know what you are doing.

Not setting goals or thinking they mean nothing is the same as saying anything or anywhere you happen to end up in life will be all right. There is no telling what you can do when you get inspired by your goals, when you believe in them. There is no telling what will happen when you act on them.

Goals direct and divert your time and energy.

Goals make the difference between living a life of dreaming and living a life of doing.

Many people in life know what they should do, but they never do it. The reason is they are lacking the drive that only a future of hope can provide. Set goals that will really push your life; they will help you create energy and direction.

Often people say they really don't have any goals. This is simply not possible. The human mind is always pursuing something, if nothing more than the ability to reduce or eliminate pain; our brains also drive us toward pleasure. Look how strong your intentions were when you were misguided and trading what wasn't real and only fleeting.

Goal Setting

We all have goals—not having any goals is a goal.

It takes a drop of inspiration to become a river of dreams

If you achieved success without a concerted and clear direction before you started using methamphetamine, *imagine what your life will be like when you commit to a strategy.* You've burned a few brain cells since then, so sticking to a plan will make your journey back easier. The good thing is if you've achieved once, you can do it again. Goals keep you focused.

Write your goals down. Goals that are not written down are merely intentions. Your ambitions have to be turned into clearly defined actions before they can be realized.

It's true that setting goals increases your risk of failure, but it also increases your chance for success. *You know where you are going when you set goals to guide you,* and you know when you're not going too, so you can adjust your aim. That doesn't mean you failed—maybe you were a little unrealistic at first.

Be specific. By setting yourself specific goals, you allow yourself to live more spontaneously, which seems ironic but is true. Without goals you can risk falling into the trap of too much time wasted on low-value, low-priority tasks and not enough on high-value, high-priority ones. Setting specific, written goals keeps you mentally focused and your energy levels high as you see your achievements.

> *Visualization is human beings' vehicle to the future;*
> *good, bad, or indifferent, it's in our control.*
> —EARL NIGHTINGALE.

ASSIGNMENT 22
HOW TO SET AND ACHIEVE YOUR GOALS

If you knew you could not fail, what would you do? If you were absolutely certain of success, what would you do, and what actions would you take?

Work through the following process:

1) Start by taking an inventory of your dreams—the things you want to do, be, and have.

All of us have some idea of the things we want. Some are vague: more love, more money, more time to enjoy life. However, to create a result, we need to become more specific than a new car, a new house, or a better job.

Referring to the **Circle of Life** you completed earlier**,** write down some of the desires, wishes, and commitments to what you would like in the areas of work and career, family and friends, health and wellbeing, community, recreation and leisure, spiritual and personal development, financial freedom, and love relationships. Don't try to figure out how you are going to achieve any of it yet.

Use the following as a guide;

a) On a large piece of paper, make an inventory or list of your dreams—the things you want to do, be and have. *There are no limits.* Use the areas in the **Circle of Life** to guide you. Be adventurous; remember your obituary. Line up the dreams you have with your drug-free life.

b) If you were to achieve these dreams, when would you do it by? Your expected time frame to begin is …? Your expected time for completion is …?

c) Choose the dreams that are most important to you. The following questions will help you choose:

- Why am I committed?
- Why is this a priority?
- Who will benefit?
- Who will I motivate to help me?

Just write it down. Knowing your outcome is the first step to achieving it.

2) Go over your list, estimating when you expect to see results.

Six months, one year, two years, five, ten, or twenty years—what is your time frame? If all your goals are short-term you need to take a longer view of potential and possibility. If all your goals are long-term, you need first to develop some steps to lead you in the direction you expect to go.

3) Choose the most important goals for you this year.

Prioritize your goals. Choose the things you are most committed to, the things that would give you the most satisfaction. Now write down *why* they are most important to you. Be clear, concise and positive. *Why you would do something is much more important than how.* Tell yourself why you are sure you can reach the results you have set for yourself.

4) Review your list of key goals

Note that if the goals are maintainable for you, are they stated positively? Are they sensory specific? Will you know when they have been reached? If they don't, change them to fit.

5) Make a list of the resources you have at your disposal.

To construct a powerful vision of your future, make a list of the things you have going for you: your character traits, friends and family support, financial resources, education, time, and energy. Your inventory will include strengths, knowledge, skills, abilities, resources, and tools.

6) Focus on the time you used some of those resources most skillfully.

Imagine four or five times when you were most successful. Write them down. Describe what you did that made you succeed, what qualities and resources you made effective use of, and what is it about the situation that made you feel successful.

7) Describe the kind of person you would have to be to achieve your goals.

Success has components to it; successful attitudes, beliefs, and behaviors determine success. *What are they?* Will it take a great deal of discipline, or more education? Take the time now to write a couple of paragraphs about the traits, skills, attitudes, and beliefs you will need to have as a person to achieve all you desire.

8) Write down what prevents you having the things you want right now.

One way to overcome the limitations you have created is to know exactly what they are. *You already know that; recognize any excuses you may be putting up, and change them now!* We can know what we want, why we want it, who will help us, and much more, but the critical factor that in the end determines whether we succeed in achieving our outcomes is our actions.

To guide your actions, you must create a step-by-step plan. You need a sequence and structure so that the actions you take complement and reinforce each other. *Now you put together your plan.*

9) What do you have to do to achieve the results you desire?

Start with your ultimate outcomes, then work backward, step by step. What are the major steps, and what can you do today, tomorrow, this week, this month, this year, to produce results? By working backward, you can map out the precise path to follow from your ultimate goal down to what you can do today. *Take each of your key goals, and create your first draft of a step-by-step plan on how to achieve it on the worksheet provided.* Make sure your plans include something you could do today—seeing family, making a phone call for information, walking, pricing an item, or buying a book.

10) Plan your ideal day.

Who would be involved? What would you do? How would it begin? Where would you go? Where would you be? How will it feel to climb into bed at the end of a day and you know you can be proud? Remember, all results, actions, and realities we experience start from our minds, so create your day the way you desire it most. *Thought precedes action.*

11) Design the perfect environment for you.

Design an environment that would bring out the best of you as a person. If you don't have a clear understanding of what your ideal day would be, what are your chances of creating it? If you don't know what your ideal environment would be, how would know what it is? **Remember, the brain needs clear, bright, intense and focused signals of what it wants to achieve.**

Final Check

Your goals need to comply with the following:;

State your goals in the positive. Decide what you want to have happen, not what you don't want. State exactly what you want.

Be as specific as possible. How does it look, feel, sound, smell? Engage all your senses in describing the results you want. The richer you make it means your brain works to create your desire. You know how that works; you've done it before, to your detriment.

Be in control. Your outcome must be initiated and maintained by you. It must not be dependent on other people having to change themselves for you to be happy. Make sure your outcome reflects things that you can affect directly.

Check that your outcome is environmentally safe and desirable. Project the consequences of your actual goal in the future. Your outcome must benefit you and other people and be socially responsible.

Have a finish line. Know how you will look, how you will feel, and what you will see and hear in your world *after you have achieved your outcome.* If you don't know when you've achieved your goal, you may already have it. You can be winning and feel like you are losing if you don't keep score. Set specific dates so you know you are on track.

If you have achieved success before, you can have it again. I know this planning is extensive and thorough, but it works.

> *Thinking is the hardest thing to do, which is the*
> *probable reason why so few engage in it.*
> —HENRY FORD

Goals are a means to an end, not the ultimate purpose of our lives. They are a tool to concentrate our focus and move us in a direction. We pursue goals so that we expand and grow. As you achieve your goals, it is *who you become* as you overcome the obstacles necessary to achieve these goals that can offer you the deepest and longest lasting sense of fulfillment.

Who you are now is somebody drug free who needs to start again, from the beginning.

ASSIGNMENT 24
WHO AM I AT MY BEST?

- What is my new best?
- Who am I when I am my best?
- What kind of person will I have to become in order to achieve all that I want, to be the best I can be?

ASSIGNMENT 25
PLANNING CHECKLIST

- What is my end goal?
- What resources/equipment do I need now?
- What will it cost me? In time? In money?
- Do I need computer skills?
- What/who can help me?
- What is the first step?
- What are the steps along the way?
- Who do I need help from to realize this dream?
- What's in it for them?
- When will I contact them?
- How will I make the time?
- What is likely to stop me?

ASSIGNMENT 26
Y DAILY HABITS

Small, constructive actions done on a daily basis will give you a sense of accomplishment and forward momentum. Start now and do simple things. No one is going to take your place here. *The small things you do make now will a big difference to your life and relationships.* If you do as you know you must and fail to recover, if you start using again, you know now that becomes a choice. *Don't let your excuse be that you didn't know what to do instead—because now you do.*

ASSIGNMENT 27
TIME AND ENERGY AUDIT

If time seems to escape you, try doing a time audit. Using a diary, record everything you do over a three-week period, on the hour, every hour. It's laborious, but if your excuse is you haven't got time, this is a way of finding some.

If it is energy you are lacking, along with the time audit, measure your energy levels. If they dip at certain times of the day, maybe it is what you are eating, or not eating. Could it be you are not exercising enough or sleeping too late? The audit will reveal all!

Questions to ask yourself when you have achieved your goal/s

- Now I have my result how do I feel?
- What was the result of my goal?
- Was the end result the same as my vision? If it was better, in what way? If it was worse, in what way?
- What could I have done differently?
- Was the effort worthwhile?
- What have I learned?

WHAT NEXT???

Anytime you like, use this prayer to help find peace.

The Lord is my shepherd; I shall not want. He makes me to lie
down in green pastures; he leads me beside the still water. He
restores my soul; He leads me in the path of righteousness for
His name's sake. Yea, though I walk through the valley of the
shadow of death, I will fear no evil; for you are with me.
—THE BIBLE PSALM 28

This guided meditation is a surrender to forgiveness and will bring you serenity.
It means you can treat yourself gently. By surrendering to forgiveness, you can
release yourself from the pain of anger, shame, and guilt.

Find a quiet place to lie or sit comfortably. Gently close your eyes, and quiet
your thoughts. Take seven deep, slow, even breaths. With each breath, relax
each muscle in your body.

Relax every single muscle in your face and neck. Then start to relax your
shoulders, arms, hands, and fingers. As you breathe deeply, slowly and evenly
move down your body and relax your chest, abdomen, and back. Relax.

Imagine a warm, golden sun. Feel the rays of the sun warming your body and
filling it with warm, gold, healing light. Now you are in a warm pool in a
quiet, peaceful surrounding. There are other people there, faces from the past,
and they are smiling at you.

Now, hear these loved ones from long ago tell you to start your day with love,
fill each day with love, and end each day knowing you are loved. Accept that
you can forgive others. Know that you are forgiven. You are completely and
absolutely and totally forgiven.

Take deep, slow, even breaths. You are completely relaxed and loved.

As you step out of the water, a master appears. He holds the wisdom of the universe
in his heart. Feel him place his hands in yours and start telling you about the great
vision and purpose for which you were born into this world. You are completely
relaxed. Know you are loved and forgiven, and you love and forgive others.

He tells you that in the serenity and stillness in your heart, your life's mission and purpose will be revealed.

Every muscle in your body is relaxed; you feel calm. You are starting to become aware of your body again. You feel so energized and ready for great things to happen today. You know you are loved; you have been forgiven and you have forgiven others.

You are refreshed, alive, and awake. Take a slow, deep breathe; open your eyes, and return to waking consciousness.

Following is a template to write your goals in. If you make a copy you can put them around to look at often. If you make copies you can give them to people who care for you and then they can help.

GOALS TEMPLATE

Here is a list of things to do to discover living again: pray, meditate, laugh, enjoy, sing, let go, accept, create, imagine, feel, consider, write, relax, radiate, help, walk, exercise, work, listen, learn, reflect, give, be thankful, share, enquire, read, appreciate, give, receive, be flexible, do something kind, contribute, volunteer, dream, plan, wish upon a star, act, forgive, celebrate, breathe, smile, be happy for someone, open your heart.

For the recovering being coached: Be prepared for hard times; they happen to all of us. Be prepared to feel frustrated, despondent, anxious, and hopeless at times, and sometimes ready to give up.

You don't use methamphetamine if you are living a well-chosen life. You use methamphetamine to fill in the gaps—but it makes holes remember.

You will get through this. ask anyone who doesn't use methamphetamine: **methamphetamine is a not prerequisite to a life worth living.** There are always consequences, and, ironically, as you challenge yourself to freedom, you have other pieces to pick up, pieces you have escaped from. Don't let them overwhelm you—*you are more important than the mess your life looks like at present.*

And now you have strategies you didn't have or use previously. They work—if you apply them.

I am not my memories; I am my dreams.
—TERRY HOLSTEIN

Being prepared for the moments of weakness, despair, and doubt minimize their impact. The following are some questions you can ask yourself to address the doubts you are experiencing, as well as affirmations and statements to stop the fear. Take yourself away from wherever you are or who you are with if it is not helping. *You are nearly there; you're doing great.*

What am I afraid of?

What will happen if I give into my fear? Have I ever been afraid before?

What are my priorities? Why?

What do I need to do today to stay free?

My reward is worth it—I will be free.

The angst and pain I feel now while recovering is only temporary. The pain I will experience if I continue to use methamphetamine will be endless.

I know what I need to stay free of methamphetamine use now and always.

Where there is no hope, the people perish.
—BIBLE

SECTION THREE

Chapter Twenty-eight
GUIDE FOR COACHES

Following is the guide for coaches. By this I mean also family, be it mother, father, sister, brother, cousin, or friend—anyone taking a hand in this recovery. From now on I will refer to the user as a client, which is a reminder to them and you that they will be free if they use the tools and strategies you offer. And it comes as no surprise for those that offer help that there is always guaranteed to be insight, revelations, and gifts for being part of this privilege. This is not reserved for, nor the exclusive domain of, professionals. Isn't that a beauty!

For further information about becoming a coach certified in this system, details about further, extensive training are included at the back of the book

This part of the book offers coaches a resource to use when working with users. Here I explain the purpose for, the rationale behind, and the expected outcome in using the tools. They are managed and to be used in sequence. Each assignment, discussion, or inventory flows on to the next discovery; as you see from the case studies, they are interpreted differently.

Some exercises are more significant to some people and are responded to very differently, as told by the stories. In the previous case study debriefs, the subject relating the story points out the tools they found most relevant, and helpful.

Here I remind you that you are working with people who have lied. Some are very accomplished liars, people who have committed crimes against others, frequently the people closest to them. They have risked everything they had to use this drug, and they have sometimes been through rehab, counseling, or psychiatric treatment, and it hasn't stopped them yet.

They may have been told that they have a genetic inheritance or illness that makes them an addict, or that they have been victim of an unhappy past, marriage, or destiny, and that's why *it* didn't work, won't work. That's why they will always crave, be addicted, and not be able to give up.

If you as the coach believe in any of those stories, then do not go any further until you change your own beliefs, because you won't be helping.

Really they have been just self-centered individuals who chose to put themselves above the law, at the cost of others' lives, and did whatever it took till they ended up here now, needing help.

Maybe that wasn't intentional, but it is true.

To be the best coach, you need to be the first to forgive them, so you can be effective. You as a coach need to be clear in your commitment to their recovery. You need to be strong when they are not. You need to believe in them when they can't, and trust that they will get through this easily.

Everybody alive wants to believe his or her life has had some meaning—it's a condition of the human spirit. As the coach you have an overview and greater understanding of your client's hopes, wishes, dreams, and expectations, so among all the stuff that isn't working, look for some moments of success and good times (drug free of course), and point them out.

We have all suffered adversity and battled obstacles. Tease out instances, incidents, and times when your client has overcome the odds to succeed.

Some people know exactly what they need to do and how, and this process is inspiring. Some people don't know where to begin, and this process is inspiring. Remember the savage nature of methamphetamine means it takes perfectly functioning, successful people down. So for some it is about making minor and quite comfortable adjustments back to success. For other people it may be everything in their life has changed.

This is also the part where I take the most common and least helpful thoughts and show you my argument that as a coach I dispel so that an immediate recovery is possible.

It is not possible if these thoughts are allowed to continue; they are the antithesis of recovery. We know how people think determines how they will act, how they act reinforces how they think.

He who fears he shall suffer already suffers what he fears.
—MONTAIGNE

USING THE TOOLS

You have started the coaching process with the **Circle of Life.** While your client is considering their thoughts about where they are in their life today, as well as their level of satisfaction, listen for beliefs that align their attitude to whether or not they align to achieving a successful recovery.

For example, in relation to health and well-being, your client may try saying, "I'm an addict; I don't have any control over my habit." Well, welcome to the saddest and most prolific excuse ever. *So how does that belief make them free? It doesn't; it keeps them using.*

Chapter Twenty-nine

METHAMPHETAMINE: THE MYTHS

Their mind is their weapon in this fight. It either limits them or frees them. One way or the other, that is the defining bit!

CHALLENGING THE DRIFT

Holding onto the thought that they are addicted traps your client into believing they have no freedom to choose, and by going with that argument, they don't. There are too many people who have used drugs and, on making a decision, turned their lives around instantly to make nonsense of such fatalistic thinking.

Your client needs to do what the people who successfully turn their lives around do: stop making excuses, shorten the process, and go straight to stop. That applies to you too, coach. No excuses.

So far, your client will have started to look at the truth in his life: he has used drugs to avoid some circumstances, hide pain, and have a great time. Methamphetamine turns ugly; so does he after he comes to terms with how he has behaved. He then has to stop blaming others people, his circumstances, genetics, and birth order, and face up.

DISPELLING MYTHS ABOUT METHAMPHETAMINE

The most significant change in immediate recovery that needs to be made in users' belief system is to move them from thinking methamphetamine is desirable to knowing meth is filthy and dangerous and will leave them with nothing but trouble.

If they don't change their minds here, then they may stop using, but only until it is too tempting and they start doing it again, or else spend a long time, often forever, desiring and craving the experience again. And that is the difference between people who do and people who don't successfully recover their lives and live free from methamphetamine use.

People choose behaviors that seem acceptable to them, and as part of our ability to think, we humans can visualize. The power to visualize is what separates us from animals. Knowing this, it is easy to change a belief that changes an action, behavior, or habit.

People do the best with what they know, and when they know more, they do better. Nice thought, but don't believe it yet. People who use methamphetamine know exactly what they are doing—that it is illegal and that they wouldn't be in such distress now if they hadn't done it more than once.

People use methamphetamine because it feels good to them at first. If it meant pouring petrol over their arms and setting them on fire before they could smoke methamphetamine, would they do that twice? I doubt it. Why? Because that would hurt them too much! If they had to weigh up between an intense, extreme pain, every time for the pleasure they got from methamphetamine, would they do it to themselves?

You think they can't see the potential for harm? They don't care. They just don't see enough reason to stop. Stop making excuses for them!

And remember, transformational change can occur in an instance. Does that happen? More often than not in my experience, how do you know? You can see it, feel it; you know it. While you stay wary, at the same time trust yourself enough to know your determination and belief in them will win, because you are backed by your tools.

When you coach a methamphetamine user, you hear stories that make you wonder how anyone decent could be so cruel, callous, deceitful, and basically evil—not in all cases, but some people. I am not part of the brigade that says these people cannot help it, so I will keep working without excuses toward stopping the supply and demand of the drug that is so insidiously involved in so much pain and suffering in any way I can.

Here's the gist: I can't help/stop using methamphetamine. I'm addicted; this drug has me in its grip, it's genetic, and I'm helpless.

How does the mind-set that says *methamphetamine is so highly addictive and the user has no free will* reconcile with anyone who has ever used methamphetamine being free? That's right; it doesn't. *What incentive does it offer users to quit? That's right; it doesn't!*

Why do we (free from methamphetamine) accept these excuses that deny our rights as their (the users) law?

The second myth that is perpetuated is, *when the user hits rock bottom, they will seek help.* That simply doesn't make sense; rock bottom means the user is at fever pitch and at a time when their need to use is most demanding. Surely that must be at the height of their compulsion, and the hardest time to stop! The minute they start using methamphetamine, they are at rock bottom.

Finally the pain of using is causing them angst, realization, and regret. *The pleasure of using has become pain; their mind-set has shifted. They are making a new decision:* there is no pleasure anymore, *the pain of using is outweighing the pleasure,* and it is innate in us as humans to avoid pain. So we do.

And we need somewhere to go with it, so use the tools, and your client will be on a guided journey to recovery.

The third myth purported by these same institutions of thought then relinquish all responsibility by saying the *user must decide whether they are ready.* Well, *is it about choice or not?* If it is, then it has nothing to do with a chemically driven and addictive nature, and anyone can stop. I think more specifically that means people make the decision as to whether they think they can stop. If the medical view says they cannot, then I guess they're the experts.

The following series of questions will challenge the thinking of people who use. Work with your client to change the beliefs that keep them using, for the mind-set that says they can stop when they want to because it is up to them to do it. I hope your client has a copy of this book and is reading it.

- What is the idea *I can't help or stop using methamphetamine* doing for my health/relationships/career, my life, and everybody involved in it who are also victims to my use?

- Is the idea *I can't help/stop using methamphetamine* helping or enhancing my life? How?
- How does what I am doing, based on the belief that *I can't help/ stop using methamphetamine,* destroy my life and others?
- How does using methamphetamine help me?
- What if I believed something different, like *I am responsible for my choices, and using methamphetamine has been a choice?*

Your client will start to realize they have been helpless to a belief that is perpetuated by systemic thinking. If they continue to stay helpless they will not stop using.

Whether you think you can, or think you can't, you're right.

—HENRY FORD

Do some research. Letters and stories sent into the Internet by users say they stopped using *when they made the decision to.* They made the decision to stop when they found enough reason to. Help them find a reason to stop and follow that up with the strategies to manage the transition.

They themselves debunk the myths of addiction—okay, it is not always easy to stop, *but it is a choice.*

These beliefs perpetuated by the medical model, are the same kind of thinking that makes stories like Lance Armstrong's fight over cancer a victory- while other people will succumb to the same disease because they have been told with authority it is incurable.

The medical experts, who promote a belief that users are not responsible/ not in control of their own will are simply reinforcing their use. Your client knows more now and they will start to feel some doubt about this kind of thinking.

CHANGING THE BELIEFS THAT KEEP YOU TRAPPED

It is easy to change a belief provided:

- You replace it with a belief you prefer.
- You keep the benefits the old beliefs gave you.

- The new belief is meaningful and congruent with your values, vision, and dreams

When your client makes any of the excuses above, take them through the following—strike while the iron is hot.

- Is the idea that *I can't stop using methamphetamine true?* Is it true under all circumstances? Does everyone believe it? If not, why not?
- Think of all the beliefs that have come and gone in medicine over the last ten years: they changed because *somebody challenged them first.*
- What would you rather believe if it was that simple?
- How will my life be better *if I believe I have control over my use of methamphetamine?*
- How might my life be worse *if I believe I have control over my use of methamphetamine?*
- What is the best thing that could happen *based on my old belief?*
- What is the best thing that could happen *based on my new belief?*
- What might stop me adopting this new belief?
- If I believe *I have control over methamphetamine use in my life,* will I be happy and get what I want?

Change the belief, change the behavior.

The coach must start with each person as if he or she were at the beginning of a new life with no doubts, and carry the utmost faith into the relationship. Like love, charisma, respect, courage, power, and trust, faith is an intangible, and your faith in your client will be evident in your actions, their responses, and your results. This model puts responsibility on you as a coach to hold the intention, not make excuses, and expect the very best outcome. Without exception and starting now, *your strength and honesty carries theirs.*

Pity arises when we are sorry for someone.
Compassion is when we understand and help wisely.
—BUDDHA

Will you be disappointed? Maybe, maybe not. As you see from the stories, people set out and do things differently. *You Are More Than This Will Ever Be* offers proven psychological strategies and offers the tools that provide the steps your client needs to take. This book promises that if your client does the work, if they make the choices necessary, then they will find the resources to stop. There is no silver bullet—it takes work. Even if all you do is sit down for the first session, you will have made an indelible mark on your client. You may be surprised just how easy it is to take somebody who is

> *We are all capable of good and evil. We are not born bad; everybody has something good inside. Some hide it, some neglect it, but it is there.*
> —MOTHER TERESA

Methamphetamine takes away decency. Methamphetamine makes people behave evilly. When they stop using meth, you can start to believe them again, and they can start to find the good in them. That will happen.

Chapter Thirty

BRING IT ON

I want my dreams back—I've been a slave to you.
You've got a hold on me.

—COMMON SENTIMENT SHARED BY METH USERS

As a coach, you may be feeling a little apprehensive. Good; there's a huge gain to be made here. Frequently my clients get sent to me against their will, and they are not happy and quite offensive.

You may start with a crappy attitude from your client. If you do, don't let it put you off. They are feeling stupid, desperate, sad, or angry, and sometimes all of the above! Whatever the emotion is, they don't deal with them well, or they wouldn't be using methamphetamine at all, would they?

An arrogant or angry attitude is one of the trademark characteristics of a methamphetamine user, and it is difficult at first. While using, they felt invincible and bullet proof and powerful.

This attitude has been a successful lie while they used, so be prepared. If they want to hold on to being arrogant because they think it gives them an edge, keep them on track with how good they will look when they have more money, freedom, and independence to develop other things they want. The reassurance you offer your client will make them strong, and once they are involved in the tools, they usually start to see what they can do to end the dissention they feel.

As a coach, you know you will meet people who are just difficult—they will always lie and cheat, be self–centered, and show no consideration toward others. You will know when the disadvantages for you to continue working with them exceed the rewards. You can set and expect certain behaviors for yourself when you work with users. You need to be clear about how it will be, just as any other family/friends who are part of this recovery. Remember, too, it is an honor to help; this person is wounded, and you can help.

If your client remains where he has been living as a user and his or her parents or partner are not aligned with your part in their recovery, they will make it difficult. Combine this with the suspicious, sometimes paranoid thinking that can plague your client, and you will be pushing it uphill all the way. In these circumstances it is better to ask your client to move away from the current environment, which will seem to them that you are placing an extra burden on them at the time.

If they stay in hostile surroundings, it will be a little tougher but not insurmountable. Sometimes there will seem no choice, but this is only another lesson in where you put your attention brings you results. *When your client focuses on alternatives, he or she will find them.*

Methamphetamine has given your client extra confidence that wasn't earned, and as things start to change for the client, it may not seem to be easy anymore, or what they want at all. They used methamphetamine when they felt sad, angry, or happy, and they got an exaggerated feeling of being able to cope. They didn't care anyway; they had instant friends and good times. That's a lot to give up, and as drugs have played such a part in their life, *replacement behaviors need to be found immediately.*

You as an observer will be looking at what seems to be a wreck at times. In the early stages, your client will hold on to their delusions of who they could be as if it was real. Methamphetamine makes people believing they can do it all, and they do: while they are smashed, they talk a lot and take outrageous risks. They cheat and lie to get more of what they want. They do not feel empathy or care for consequence; as long as they get what they want, they will do whatever it takes.

Their ego needs are high, and their self-esteem is low. Ego needs driveyour user for things, to look good and now, to feel good immediately and at any cost. Ego needs aare externally focused and results based. Methamphetamine is a cheats way to meeting ego –driven needs, but it is a shallow empty accomplishment,

A sense of self-esteem is what you earned by the things you have done for others; the kindness you offer; the respect you show; and the feelings of love, oneness, and belonging. Your client hasn't been doing much of that, so their self-esteem is pretty dented and is a reason to not feel too good, while their ego is screaming at them to appear they are top on their game, remember they need to justify their use The tools work because they immediately start to identify your clients strength's, dreams and desires so use them.

The difference in this model is it treats each person individually; while it is a system and theoretically sound, it allows for personal problems and solutions.

This is not an elaborate process; it is simple and proven, and addresses the user's unique and individual past, then quickly starts your client seeing opportunities.

Check that your client is able to read and write. If not, use discussion, and take the notes yourself.

Chapter Thirty-one

Alarm, Motivate, and Inspire

The first tool is the Circle of Life, a self-analysis tool. The client sees their life in a holistic way; they review and rate their life to their own standards and compare it only to their own expectations and how they understand the world.

Session 1 takes at least three hours; your goal as coach is to alarm, inspire, and motivate.

The client measures his levels of satisfaction in all areas of their lives; when he has rated all areas, get him to define each area as to what it means to him—for example, use "Health and Wellbeing." A good range of questions to ask are "What does good health and well-being mean to you? What does it take you to maintain a good level of health in your life? How do you maintain your level of health and wellbeing?" From the responses you can gauge the attitude and beliefs he holds. For some people, not being sick is good health; for others, they may have always been very fit and strong, and expect it always to be like that, but first you must ask and understand what it means to each person.

Then by asking, "What does it take to stay that way?" your client must address the way he is living today. Is he doing the things he used to—exercising, eating well, sleeping for optimum performance?

Maybe he has always had shaky habits. One thing you know for sure is his care for himself has taken a dive—after all, methamphetamine has red lye, battery acid, and strychnine in it - how can that be healthy?

If your client exposes any health concerns, as his coach you can prompt him into getting the medical attention he needs. Ask him when he will go to the doctor, and get him to call you when he has been.

The Circle of Life is a truthful enquiry into a person's life. Do not expect him to be happy with where his life is now—people take drugs to replace feeling sad, angry, lonely; to dull pain; to feel more powerful, invincible, and successful. There are many and varied interpretations of living; find out what his expectations are in his own words to start to truly understand him.

> *Our deepest fears are like dragons guarding our greatest treasures.*
> —RAINER MARIA RILKE

Not even the most arrogant of the clients I remember having felt life was where they wanted it to be after completing the Circle of Life at the first session.

The next questions are related to where or what he would like any specific areas in his life to be like. Frequently your client has managed to avoid such honesty for a while now, and this is often a clear and brutal reality check. After all, it is only based on his own expectations. There is no one making him right or wrong, or judging him—the process has started; he is doing that.

A good technique is to start with a question like, "What is the greatest area of concern in your life?" Generally your client will start with what is most important to him. It is important to see through the false optimism, half-truths, lies, and illusions. How do you know he is telling you a porkie? Does what he say sound plausible?

Setting assignments and asking questions starts to establish a level of reciprocity. Does he keep to the agreement he has with you? Is he where he said he would be? Does he take the time to write his assignments? Dig down; search for congruency in the story and the facts. How can a person say his behavior did not affect his family if he is not home or smashed at night, if money is being spent on drugs? How can he report good health if he is using? Call the bluff!

Is it hurting enough yet? You are working with people who are committing crimes, at least one. It needs to hurt them to keep using.

Something to keep in mind here is the client frequently feels elated by the end of the first session. Someone has listened to him; he as talked about himself and has been heard. He believes it will be easy, it's what he wants, it's for the best, done deal. Don't let your determination waiver, succumb, or become complacent. People who are using methamphetamine tell lies, exaggerate, and are invincible … and on the other hand, you may have just instigated a change for life that will last forever.

In the midst of your illness, you will promise a goat, but when you have recovered, a chicken will seem sufficient.
—JUKIN SAYING, FROM
THE LITTLE BOOK OF AFRICAN WISDOM

The intention of the first session is to instigate a change that will last forever. Don't let anyone tell you he is not ready. If he is not now, keep giving him more reasons to be.

What he is doing by using methamphetamine makes him part of a trade that has far-reaching and painful consequences. Don't let him off the hook, coach.

The Circle of Life is used at every session—it is a graphic representation, and progress can be seen in all areas. While the user concentrates on just one aspect, by symbiosis, other areas improve too. It illustrates the fact that it takes being fully aware and attentive to old habits, behaviors, and thinking, and there will be noticeable consequences one way or another. *It holds a picture of promises broken and shows the way it is and the way it could be.*

The Circle of Life is a tool to clarify your client's belief systems: how he thinks, what his thinking is based on, what his expectations are. It explains why he does what he does. Sometimes, though not always, *drug use is a direct result of having seen drug use as an acceptable behavior.* The user believes it to be an escape from pain, life, and responsibility. Sometimes taking drugs is the polar opposite to how he lived and learned as a child. This is a game with no rules, and it doesn't make sense as to why anyone would endure parents or caregivers as drug users and then do the same to themselves and their kids. As much as it doesn't make any sense for a person, who was given a healthy and happy life as a child, to become a user and let her life, and anyone else involved, get out of control.

Don't let them ply you with excuses about it being too hard. That is all they are: excuses.

After doing the Circle of Life, it will be obvious to you that there are thoughts patterns here that are not constructive and need to be changed. First they must be challenged with the following questions:

- Where did you learn that?
- Why are you so sure?
- What other options are there?
- Would you do it differently next time?
- What would you do instead?

When you ask good, inquiring questions, you provoke your client into having to think and formulate their answers, challenging their knee-jerk reactions and making them search for what they know.

Your commitment as coach to their recovery/discovery is tantamount here. Change your thoughts, change your world . Your own life will be looking pretty tremendous by now; that's the gift in helping others.

Chapter Thirty-two
UNDERSTANDING THE ASSIGNMENTS

The following is a précis of each assignment and the expected outcomes.

Assignment 1, Circle of Life. Assignments are a key tool for the client to facilitate growth and discovery. They ensure reciprocity, and the client's commitment to the developing relationship can be seen by their readiness to complete them.

Assignment 2, Your Values. Having to define them reminds her who she used to be or could be. You teach children values by teaching them to obey rules, keep agreements, and comply with legislation that is put in place to keep society safe. It's time to renew those values by discovering what they are, because your client hasn't been doing much in the way of keeping rules and agreements or obeying laws that keep us all safe.

Assignment 3, 10 Defining Moments in Your Life and **Assignment 4, Seven People Who Made a Difference,** show how influential certain times and people have been in her life, who they are, and what made them. Both these essays ask your client to take a retrospective glance backward, which is necessary to go forward.

Assignment 5, Knowledge, Skills, and Abilities, is a reminder that life has not been wasted and that your client has talents and skills to use now.

Assignment 6, This Is Your Life, is the beginning of a dream. Imagine having the complete freedom to decide what you do for the rest of your life. You do! This is to be completed over the first week by the client. Is it easy to do? Not by everybody. But is it essential? Yes; it brings back hope. Without hope, life is just too hard and desolate. Hope is the first resolution we make, when we know we can trust and the world is a good place.

Assignment 7, How Did I Get Here, reveals patterns—your client's strategies, or lack of them. This is a summary of circumstances where lifetime patterns, experiences, and events are recorded. Your client will reveal to herself defining moments, things she wishes she had done, and things she wishes she hadn't.

As coach, your job is to observe patterns and behaviors that are both resourceful and not, decisions that were wise and unwise; to calibrate her mind-set and attitudes at the time; and to understand, in combination with her Circle of Life, her expectations.

Methamphetamine can leave users feeling depressed, agitated, and violent, which then leads to a downward spiral of behavior and demand for more. Often users have lost their families or inevitably are about to, along with jobs, money, possessions, health, and pride. Let's face it: their behavior has been pretty bad up until now. Isn't it true that the best line of defense is a good offense? They are in attack–*just don't let it be you* or other irrelevancies.

Scapegoats and red herrings are all the distractions and excuses that help them stay where they were.

While the past is gone, this is a valuable insight into how things happened the way they did, and the best strategy for initiating change. Two questions that are vital are, What have you done to get where you are right now? What do you want to be different?

Knowledge is king!

Assignment 8, Blocks, Red Herrings, and Sabotage, is a call to be honest and reveal all the excuses and self-limiting beliefs she uses. This challenges your client to become accountable for the things she has done without thinking and her lack of achievement so far. Your client will gain insight into the way she typically behaves, usually how she justifies her behavior and blaming others. This will reveal any limitations and patterns she may have accepted as reality. They will gain an understanding of the thoughts and beliefs they hold. Lead your client into taking a new perspective toward where they have come from, that can change now!

The way the client approaches the assignment provides the coach with information about what the client feels is and isn't possible, building on the information gathered through the personal profiling, the obituary, and what the client has verbally communicated.

Assignment 9, Challenge, Change, and Succeed, focuses your client's attention on what to do about how she has been living up until now, *now that they know more.*

Frequently we have accepted and adopted thoughts without challenging them. This assignment is designed to query old patterns of thoughts and behaviors once more, reveal excuses that your client is still using, and, knowing how resourceful your client is, start to look for alternatives.

Holding onto old patterns of thinking and being makes us human. We go with what we know because of two things: it's all we know, and we don't know what to do for things to be different; and we like it that way and don't want it to be different.

The tools offer the help your client needs to make a decision knowing what it will take, how it will be achieved, and who will be with her on the journey.

Don't baby your client—she knows exactly what she is doing!

Assignment 10, Love Will Set You Free. When your client starts to tell the truth, live with values, achieve small things along with the biggie (staying drug free), it is inevitable she will start a new love affair with herself.

Assignment 11, Promises, Promises, is an agreement to keep others safe, complying with rules, and beginning to live her values.

The **Health and Wellbeing Self-Evaluation** is important for your client to address any health concerns she may have, and to get in touch again with looking after herself. Remember, the consequences of using methamphetamine are severe for some people, and they will suffer anxiety attacks and episodes of sadness. There are lots of clues there about exercise and relaxation.

Assignment 13, Stress Check, asks for your client's specific coping strategies: what she does now to manage stress instead of turning to drugs.

Assignment 14, An Account of My Life, is about knowing life hasn't always been the way you want it to be; it is your responsibility now.

Assignment 15, Results in My Life So Far, leads you to today, which may highlight how much your client has lost through using methamphetamine. Good! Things can only get better.

Assignment 16, Be Grateful for What You've Got, is about learning to be grateful again. The list will grow as the weeks go by. Being grateful paints a picture of hope returning, greater accountability, and a future worth having.

Assignment 17, Financial Health Check, is a way of taking measurable stock of what you have left financially and putting your business in order. The phoenix rises! This determines your client's viewpoints in relation to getting and staying well; once again, it is for you to challenge beliefs that will hurt your client's recovery.

Assignment 18 is a physical **Exercise in Forgiveness.** Your client has reason to forgive herself and others for things she has done or has had done to her. We all do, all the time—it's part of living. Forgiving others comes after your client forgives herself because, if she doesn't, she will feel guilty and punish herself, and start using methamphetamine again because that promised her invincibility and shut her feelings off. If she remains overwhelmed by guilt she will not recover effectively.

Assignment 19 ;You and Your Community. Recovery means reclaiming and reinventing their life and lifestyle. There will be apologies to be made, their children may have suffered too much or your client might need a complete new start. Community is crucial to feeling accepted and part of something bigger. Your client can volunteer with any time they have, their children can play team sports, they can help at schools and then there is a work community. These are the simple techniques that work.

Assignment 20, Characteristics of Successful People, gives you, the coach, another look at how the client sees her strengths and where she is weak. It also gives you an insight into her increasing levels of self-esteem, competence, initiative, and worth. These are self-assessments—your client doesn't have to compare herself or hers life with anyone else.

Assignment 21, Attitude Is Everything. Rating your attitude offers another baseline or benchmark for to client to aspire to.

Assignment 22, How to Set and Achieve Your Goals. Goals give our lives direction because they clarify our thoughts, carve our intentions, and focus our behaviors. *Your client has already named a whopper: to get free of meth use.* Setting specific goals act as a reminder, guide, and checklist. Before, during, and after recovery from meth use, your client has many things she must do to be able to stay free as easily as possible. She will suffer the usual challenges: threats we all face, but exacerbated by the lifestyle she has just had to leave. She has to get back to stable ground.

Remember also, people use drugs for many reasons. This may not be the only drug she is using; on the other hand, she may have never used drugs before. However, there are strong links with drug use and poor life-coping strategies. The tools provide an increasing new repertoire and a guide for the next time things get difficult—meth does not have to be the only option.

Assignment 23, My Inventory of Dreams, Goals, and Commitments. Goals act as a guide to make things easier: when things are going well, we get on; when times are tough, it is easy to give up. It's no secret: things are going to be tough sometimes.

One thing is certain: it gets tougher if you get caught doing methamphetamine.

The difference for people who successfully choose and achieve being free is what they do to attain it.

The people who fail recovery are those that give up at the first point of not knowing what to do next.

Traditional drug rehab usually means you sit with a counselor, lingering too long over the past, regurgitating too much misery, and presenting and seeing only the problem of the moment. Instead, let these tools preempt and circumnavigate the next eventuality before it happens. Give your client the tools to cope with, and the insight to see what is next and what can be done about it. Based on a new understanding about who she is, how she became who she did, and what to do for things to be better,

Assignment 24, Who Am I at My Best? A personal perspective from your client at this point related to her aspirations and it should look quite hot!

Assignment 25, Planning Checklist. Yes, more questions! The goal setting procedures are very thorough!

Assignment 26, My Daily Habits. Check out your habits. What are you doing all day? How much is automatic, and how much is reminiscent of when you used methamphetamine? Are you exercising, reading, and working? What are you doing without thinking? what have you slipped into because you are still living like a user?

Assignment 27, Time and Energy Audit. By taking an audit of your client's time and activity, you also see her habits and daily behaviors that most often need to change.

Expect your client to need sleep at first because her body is exhausted from the state of high-adrenaline that meth causes. The sooner she gets herself back to a healthy lifestyle timetable, the better she will feel and the easier the return. Using meth causes a decrease in appetite and, in recovery, an increased desire for carbohydrates and sugar, so it is important for your client to start eating fresh fruit and vegetables because of the weight gain often experienced.

Recovery is about replacing behaviors that are habitual, and your client cannot take away such a huge chunk of behavior and not replace it. That would leave a hole in her mental universe. New actions have to be put in place, so in order to change the habitual behaviors she does every day, we must first discover what she is doing with time and then do different things. Why? Because automatic behavior leads to a state of unconscious reflex action lifestyle, and decisions are made automatically, without any thought put into them.

Users are people who have been in the habit of staying up all night, sitting and talking for days on end. They miss this. If time is not consciously altered and new things scheduled, they will stick to the old times, and nothing will have changed for them, except what they believe as having being taken away. There's the hole—it has to be filled.

If your client is on home detention or house arrest, it is more difficult to offer new activities to replace the old. Ironically, she is in a more similar position as previously when using at home like this, than they would be if they were free to start work. Your client is more tempted to have old friends she smoked with turn up, because she is bored—and she'll start doing it again. Stop that from happening by stopping anyone who you know still uses from visiting—they are not that much of a friend, and a threat to call the police if you see them will usually work.

Assignment 28, Questions to Ask When You Have Achieved Your Goals, is just one really: what next?

A Prayer will help your client find inner calm and feel supported and not alone.

A Meditation will soothe your client.

Chapter Thirty-three

TRICKS OF THE TRADE

HOW TO MANAGE DEPRESSION IN YOUR RECOVERING CLIENT

The effects of using methamphetamine can mean the user is more inclined to hit the ground hard, feel more desperate, and have more suicidal thoughts. Let's put it in perspective: he is no doubt still a little ashamed.

And on awakening from this escape, he should feel ashamed—that shows he is a decent person and will do what is required to make it better again.

These old thoughts, negative feelings, and lack of resilience are the same ones that got him into this mess. Change his thoughts by focusing his thinking onto the hopes and dreams he has uncovered in the Circle of Life. That changes how he feels. *There will be moments of desperation, but who doesn't have those?*

Just because the medical people tell you this will happen doesn't make it necessarily such an inevitable threat to recovery, and certainly not to your client! It means welcome to life, and your client has discovered new coping skills as he has worked through the tools, revealing his determination, resilience, and new direction.

As long as it is not life threatening, talk him through his depressive thoughts. It is a good sign; it means your client is starting to feel again. It's still self–centered, however, and while it's all about him, he won't think of anybody or anything else.

Depressive thinking signals hopelessness—he is not hopeless anymore if he is not using; he was hopeless when he was, though.

Often people have feelings of being overwhelmed and out of control—they probably are, as they haven't chosen the most resourceful strategies in the recent past, so their coping skills are negligible, and they need a hand.

Here are prepared answers and strategies to put in place if these fears raise their ugly heads.

"It will always be this way," "It always happens to me," and "I can't do anything about it" together lead to a spiral of downward thinking. These three thoughts promote helplessness and a feeling of no hope and no impetus for change.

Challenge the following three thoughts that lead to depression following use by using the following rejoinders.

It'll always be this way. What is "this way"? What is "always"? Can you remember when it wasn't always like this? Was there a time when things didn't happen this way? The appropriate assignment to use here is "Knowledge Skills, and Abilities." This is an assignment that reminds your client he has an accumulation of talents, resources, and accomplishments already available to him, as well as options for it to be different.

It always happens to me. This didn't just happen; you did it, so now do something different. "Blocks, Red Herrings, and Sabotage" challenges your client's helplessness, reminds him of habitual patterns, and kicks his butt to do something different. "Goal Setting" sets his direction.

I can't do anything about it. Yes, you can. In fact, you are the only person who can change things for yourself, and you have scientifically proven tools— use them. They are "Circle of Life," "Excuses," "Results in My Life So Far," "Be Grateful for What You've Got," and "This Is Your Life," to start with.

To the self-centered user, as long as he refers only to his own situation, nothing will look as bad or worse as his own predicament. It is no surprise, then, why meth users hang together: it stops them feeling guilty about their own actions, and there is always someone doing worse than they are. Never is the time better to be developing and increasing his awareness of his life as it is, knowing it will get better because he has made a decision to stop using methamphetamine.

Each of these exercises develops a growing rapport, relationship, and understanding, the coach discerning the client's perceptions, expectations for himself, and the most effective learning and communication style to use with him.

Chapter Thirty-four
PROCEDURES, HAPPINESS, PEACE, AND SUCCESS

This chapter gives you some suggestions about procedures. If you are doing this yourself, you are the client I refer to. It leads your client to discovering for themselves the answers to their lives, puts in place strategies based on their own choices, and gives guidance through the structure that comes from doing the assignments and exercises that will direct and focus the necessary steps they take to get back what they lost.

Coaching is an art and skill, and you can train further with me to become certified as a coach, should you wish to continue as a professional in this life-changing business.

It starts here: you have an acquaintance, friend, son, lover, or daughter who needs help. They may have refused help, thinking you don't know about it, and they may believe there is nothing they can't handle. Sometimes they have confided in you; other times they have vehemently denied anything wrong. Sometimes they get mad at you so you will back off. Sometimes they are grateful and know they are on the way to the help they need to stop this out-of-control lifestyle they are in. Don't hesitate; you could save a life by speaking.

Your client has confided they need help before it gets worse. There is a point when people know they are losing control and they start asking.

This system does not tolerate "just a little," which is a common thread among drug and alcohol clinics. Using these tools, the user does not have to go anywhere or stop their employment; they do not have to be ready to change, or willing! Have the courage to just get in front of them.

We would not have survived as a species if self-destruction was our quest. It isn't, and when people are destroying their minds, bodies, and souls, they are not having fun. Methamphetamine impacts on all of us, so why should their choice to mess up their world mess up mine, my children, and my grandchildren's legacy?

These tools will challenge your clients use, offer new behavioral choices, and lead your client back to living fully without screwing themselves over with methamphetamine.

These tools help you find peace, love, happiness, and success – they take application and it is worth it.

Confirm the client has all your contact details. This means they call you if they feel tempted, not anybody who will excuse their weakness of the moment—because it is only a moment. One of the reasons attributed to an easy recovery is having somebody there when the recovering person needs them. The right support can make it easy not to go somebody who can do him or her wrong, or back down the same track, which has been the quickest escape up until now.

This is only a suggestion, and it is not your responsibility, so if and when it suits, it helps if you are available. If you are not available, he or she will need to find someone who is. A reminder; your client may not have sought help from anywhere or anyone else, so consider it a privilege to be helping them.

Don't wait for the perfect time. The first session is crucial for you as a coach. This is your chance to make an impact with your use of the tools that are very simple and can be used anywhere. Make sure that you are as comfortable as possible, with a degree of privacy and safety. You have the tools; clarify your own intention, and enjoy.

Make an agreement that you will work together for eight sessions, then further by negotiation. Keeping agreements and living within parameters is the first promise they make to themselves again.

The first session is the Circle of Life. Draw it in front of your client, asking them for the things they believe make up their life, and then fit them into the existing categories.

Follow that with "Your Values," "10 Defining Moments," "7 Influential People," and "Knowledge, Skills, and Abilities." That will take about three hours. This is an exploratory session—even if you think you knew this person well before, you will know them a lot better after this, and so will they. Keep the paperwork so they can't lose it or forget it. Give them a copy of this book to read, even if they say they don't read. Someone close will pick it up. It is your back-up.

Remember, your strength and commitment will carry them. A feeling of hope for the future is your outcome today, coach!

If you get through the session, you will have made an indelible mark in your client's life and their expectations. Set them their assignment, "This is Your Life," and a new time to meet. I suggest within two days.

Midway between sessions: Call the client (yes I know sometimes they have no phone, or are in prison; work around those nuisances) and ask him to bring a diary. Have a spare one in case he doesn't, and bring your sense of humor.

The second session is a review; let your client speak. Just be nice; they are usually quite excited and pleased, or angry and don't want to see you. It's the same thing really, just different ends of the behavioral spectrum. *They will not be indifferent.* If they act like they are, they don't mean it.

Wow, you've got a relationship going!

You might start a Time/Energy Audit. The question "What are you doing with your wild and precious life?" makes him think life is wild and precious and worthwhile—it is!

He is detoxing and needs reminders about eating properly, and so "Health and Well-being" is a good place to start. Go for a walk with him; act as a scribe if he hasn't written the homework assignment. Watch a new life unfold. Have you noticed we haven't lingered on what was wrong, bad or stupid!

So far what we have done is shown our client trust, respect, and an interest in him. You have expected the same from your client. This is how easy it is!

Session two review: Just enjoy the feeling. Your client will be shaky; it has been three days. He is more than the mess his life looks like at the moment. Stay strong.

Session three can be scheduled within the next two days; reality has truly set in. He has concerns and feels guilty, sad, angry, or desperate.

Great! It will never be the same for your client again. Your job is to remind him of that. There will be plenty of people around him who will not be helping.

Your client may be working. Clients who are managing their transition from methamphetamine use while he continues to work need as stress-free an environment as possible. It means your sessions need to focus on his roles and responsibilities in the workplace so he is less likely to lose it. If he remains competent and manages his relationships without stress, he will work through without any disturbance. It's a good idea for your client to take a few days off in the first week to concentrate on his exercise and eating.

Go to the Circle of Life; any changes? What are they, and why? The practical things he can do to get through this time are to exercise, sleep at night, and eat well, as covered in "Health and Wellbeing." "Blocks, Red Herrings, and Sabotage" is a strong challenge. "Promises, Promises" is a good follow-up—now we're really getting serious. "An Exercise in Forgiveness" feels good here.

Observe your client's behavior, presentation, and demeanor. Are they okay? How is his family coping? Who is he seeing? How is his "Time and Energy Audit"? Review it. Is he doing what you ask? That is what is important. You are enjoying a relationship of reciprocity. What have you achieved today? You have built more trust in someone who has been missing it. Money can't buy that!

Session three review: Your client has had seven hours of coaching so far. Family members will need to talk to you—they will be unravelling by now; they have trusted him before and don't want to be disappointed. Make sure they can get hold of you and express their fears to you, because you can counter them. If they don't know what you are doing, they will feel you are excluding them. *Tell them to buy this book!*

Session four starts with a look at the Circle of Life. Your client's life is changing. They may have to get out of where they are; they may be threatened by previous suppliers who are watching their source of money drying up. This is often a point in coaching where two things occur: your client is feeling pressure from old contacts, and he is feeling resistant.

Ask your client to complete "How Did I Get Here? An Account of My Life" and/ or "Results in My Life So Far." These are all self-revealing—no more excuses.

At about this point, your client feels invincible and unstoppable, and believes he is completely able to do it alone—he wouldn't have come to you in the first place if he could change a lifetime's habits in two or three sessions. You may have to insist on the agreement you have in place, but don't use it as control. It's an agreement.

Just ask them how things will be different if they give up on themselves now.

If you are still getting in front of him, he is getting better.

New behaviors, like sticking to agreements, need to be trialed, tested, and proved. It's not hard when you start with small challenges like establishing the next session time in advance. Keep your expectations big!

When your client procrastinates and wants to wait, avoid, or ignore you until he is ready, turn up anyway.

Session 5: Move into the "How to Set and Achieve Goals" exercise. It is very thorough and may take three sessions, but it will always be in progress.

Discuss the changes in your client's life in all areas—personal and spiritual development, love relationships, family and friends, work and career, health and well-being, love relationships, community development—using the

As things get better in one area, they get better in all areas You can expect a lot of success by this time, with plenty of discussion from your client. You will observe lots of change in your client's life. He will be looking happier, and his skin and eyes will be clearer.

At this time, there may be painful consequences to face up to. Your client may have to arrange payment of debts, apply for new custodial arrangements, start a new career, or find another place to live. Building spiritual strength through searching, prayer, and meditation is soothing in this search.

Start every day with Prayer or Meditation.

Expect your client's use of methamphetamine to be a thing of the past. Awesome!

Following sessions: Keep working through the tools; there are plenty! The following sessions will be built around new successes measured by the client using their Circle of Life. There will be areas of concern that are obvious now. Use the "Financial Health Check" and "Attitude Check" exercises, and don't forget "Be Grateful for What You've Got," "Stress Check," and "Affirmations."

Keep your client on track. Check that his goals and what he is doing with his time is in congruence.

You may negotiate further time at week eleven or twelve if necessary. This is a good time for you, as the coach, to revisit all assignments, achievements, new strategies, and decisions.

How do you feel now?

What was the outcome? I love to hear stories of courage and triumph. Please email me through my website.

P.S. Hey, coach: if you think one person is too insignificant to make a difference, have you ever spent a dark night in a room with a mosquito?

If you would like to train and certify as a coach with me, please contact www.ultimatecoachgroup.com for more information.

Methamphetamine
not now, not ever.

Author's Epilogue

I hope *You Are More Than This Will Ever Be* has helped you tackle the drug that promised you so much before it did damage to your life. I hope I provided enough information to make your decision to be free from methamphetamine use unshakeable. I hope you can make up with your friends and family, and that they like you, can put the past behind them, and trust into the future.

If you are a friend or family member I hope reading this book has helped you strengthen your beliefs that your loved one can fight this drug and now.

People who get trapped into using methamphetamine do so because they want what it promises. Methamphetamine tells lies, taking away the user's own ability to have what it promises, and more. Methamphetamine does not make you powerful, charismatic, and invincible. It is not a fast track to success—only you, drug free, can do that.

If you have coached somebody using these tools, you can be assured you have done all it takes to fight the lies and stories people told themselves to justify using methamphetamine. You have helped them get their lives back and stopped more damage to others close to them.

Because crime and methamphetamine use are so inexcusably proven to be related, your community is safer. Because of you, there will be reduced harm to innocent victims, and less children will suffer the loss of their parents to prison terms. Fewer families will be torn apart, and an enormous amount of damage to the environment will be spared.

> *Think global; act local.*
> JOHN LENNON

We have a problem with methamphetamine that is causing an unprecedented destructiveness around the world and across all economic and cultural divides. Surely now we have no choice but to address such wide-scale, pervasive, and dangerous behavior; it is affecting us all.

What is your specific responsibility? Whatever you are prepared to do, do you make a difference? As a coach to that person's life. you did: you made a difference to their loved ones, their communities, our environment, and the future. You rock!

There can be no halfway measures with methamphetamine. The supply and demand must be stopped because this drug does damage to all of us. Let's stop the demand. We can do this by saving one person at a time, sending a strong preventative message, and presenting an unrelenting refusal to believe there is nothing we can do about it. Refuse to believe we are helpless to stop this.

Training as a coach in this system is inspiring, not only in coaching users of methamphetamine, but any drug, alcohol, or behavior where people have sought help and not found the right approach—yet!

If you would like to be part of a campaign to provide real information to young people and their communities, please contact me at www.hopeofanation.net to be involved in our campaign.

The campaign is a series of live concerts, targeting thirteen-year-olds and up with a preventative message: "methamphetamine: not now, not ever." It is an exciting and crucial message delivered with a multimedia approach. The message is inspiring and direct. Local icons, performers, and athletes will take part. We deliver statistics, facts, and information in a powerful presentation, providing answers to questions, and a branded instant retort:

methamphetamine
not now, not ever

If you live in a community; belong to a church or school that would benefit; and would like your kids from thirteen years old and upward to know more, know what to say, and break the cycle because they understand the dangers, contact me through my website, and we can work together, as a global community, to provide the information that will disturb, inform, and provide enough impetus to stop methamphetamine from looking desirable. Ever.

BUY A SHARE OF THE FUTURE IN YOUR COMMUNITY

These certificates make great holiday, graduation and birthday gifts that can be personalized with the recipient's name. The cost of one S.H.A.R.E. or one square foot is $54.17. The personalized certificate is suitable for framing and will state the number of shares purchased and the amount of each share, as well as the recipient's name. The home that you participate in "building" will last for many years and will continue to grow in value.

Here is a sample SHARE certificate:

THIS CERTIFIES THAT

YOUR NAME HERE

HAS INVESTED IN A HOME FOR A DESERVING FAMILY

1985-2005

TWENTY YEARS OF BUILDING FUTURES IN OUR
COMMUNITY ONE HOME AT A TIME

1200 SQUARE FOOT HOUSE @ $65,000 = $54.17 PER SQUARE FOOT
This certificate represents a tax deductible donation. It has no cash value.

YES, I WOULD LIKE TO HELP!

*I support the work that Habitat for Humanity does and I want to be part of the excitement! As a donor, I will receive periodic updates on your construction activities but, more importantly, I know my gift will help a family in our community realize the dream of homeownership. **I would like to SHARE in your efforts against substandard housing in my community!** (Please print below)*

PLEASE SEND ME _____ SHARES at $54.17 EACH = $ $_____

In Honor Of: _____

Occasion: (Circle One)   HOLIDAY   BIRTHDAY   ANNIVERSARY

      OTHER: _____

Address of Recipient: _____

Gift From: _____ *Donor Address:* _____

Donor Email: _____

I AM ENCLOSING A CHECK FOR $ $_____ PAYABLE TO HABITAT FOR HUMANITY OR PLEASE CHARGE MY VISA OR MASTERCARD *(CIRCLE ONE)*

Card Number _____ Expiration Date: _____

Name as it appears on Credit Card _____ Charge Amount $ _____

Signature _____

Billing Address _____

Telephone # Day _____ Eve _____

PLEASE NOTE: Your contribution is tax-deductible to the fullest extent allowed by law.
Habitat for Humanity • P.O. Box 1443 • Newport News, VA 23601 • 757-596-5553
www.HelpHabitatforHumanity.org

LaVergne, TN USA
18 December 2009
167584LV00003B/88/P

9 781600 376221